ROB NIJSSE

GLASS IN STRUCTURES

ELEMENTS
CONCEPTS
DESIGNS

Foreword by MVRDV

BIRKHÄUSER
Publishers for Architecture
Basel · Berlin · Boston

Layout and cover design: Alexandra Zöller, Berlin

This book is also available in a German language edition.
(ISBN 3-7643-6440-8)

A CIP catalogue record for this book is available from
the Library of Congress, Washington D.C., USA

Bibliographic information published by Die Deutsche Bibliothek
Die Deutsche Bibliothek lists this publication in the Deutsche
Nationalbibliografie; detailed bibliographic data is available in the
Internet at <http://dnb.ddb.de>.

© 2003 Birkhäuser – Publishers for Architecture, P.O.Box 133,
CH-4010 Basel, Switzerland
A member of the BertelsmannSpringer Publishing Group
Printed on acid-free paper produced from chlorine-free pulp. TCF ∞
Printed in Germany
ISBN 3-7643-6439-4

9 8 7 6 5 4 3 2 1   www.birkhauser.ch

Contents

Please, no visible construction!

Why glass? In order to achieve the transparency that many structures require. But furthermore, the use of glass invariably produces surprises: Glass generates a great variety of unexpected effects which even the experienced designer will only partly anticipate. In my view it is not just the transparency but the sense of wonder by which architects and engineers are inspired to use glass in unconventional ways: the effect of concealment and illusion – a characteristic quality of glass which yet evades any attempt at calculation and which no drawing can convey.

Jordi Bernardo's view of the Fondation Cartier in Paris reflects this illusionary moment. The glass is seemingly not present; interior and exterior merge without a boundary between them. The architecture has moved into the background. Only the familiar bird stickers betray that the photographer has shot the view from the inside to the outside, and that the old building, which seems to be in the yard, is in reality across the street. Is this deceptive effect simply an unforeseeable spin-off or the result of a precise calculation? Should we continue to strive for transparency – or instead concentrate on the unpredictable qualities?

"Glass in Structures" shows a great number of highly inventive glass constructions and their complicated detailing. It presents the objectives as well as the potential of the structural use of glass. The angle taken is that of the structural engineer whose view, in analyses of buildings and their architecture, is often not adequately represented. The described projects are adventure stories from the world of building technology, some lead to the realization of amazing constructions, others have remained unrealised. Even in the latter cases the sense of adventure is kept, however, and the insights and experience reaped prepare us for the next expedition. The desire to explore new routes and unknown combinations characterizes every one of the projects and solutions presented. The book takes a close look at the various phases of the design process and reflects on the cooperation between architects and structural engineers.

MVRDV/Jacob van Rijs

INTRODUCTION

"I cannot tell how I shall make it but I will make it."

George Stephenson (1781 – 1848)

Glass is a fascinating material. It combines remarkable and even contradictory properties. You can look through it, and yet water, which penetrates almost everything, cannot pass through it. On the one hand it is strong and almost unbreakable, on the other hand one scratch lets it break easily.

The quest to introduce this material into the world of structural engineering has only been going on for a few decades, but it is my sincere conviction that in another few decades people will regard structural glass as trustworthy as nowadays, for instance, steel and reinforced concrete. One should not forget that steel/iron as building material is only about 200 years old and concrete even only about 100 years. (Ill. 1)

Especially the property of transparency is a valued feature of glass. The combination of being protected from rain, wind and cold and still be able to see what is going on in the outside world is in fact an ideal combina-

Ill. 2: Aquarium, Barcelona.
A large-scale tunnel allowing people
to walk safe and dry under water.

Ill. 1: Coalbrookdale Bridge:
The first all-iron bridge built in 1789.

tion. Dangerous animals on land or even from the sea can be looked at through a thick glass panel without direct danger. (Ill. 2) And even in deep space, glass allows a view on astronomical phenomenons.

Since the discovery of glass this magic property has fascinated mankind. The first form in which men met glass were the rock crystals found in mountain caves. (Ill. 3) The resemblance to ice is striking, and the fact that rock crystal does not melt must have looked like sorcery to primitive man. Then people learned how to make glass. How this, probably, was done is best illustrated by a story mentioned by the Roman writer Plinius the Elder in his magnum opus "Historia Naturalis":

"The river (Belus in nowadays Lebanon) is muddy but deep, only revealing its sands when the tide retreats. The sand does not glisten until it has been tossed about by the waves and its impurities removed. Then, and only then, when the sand is thought to have been cleansed by the scouring action of the sea, it is ready for use. The beach extends for not more than a half a mile, but for many years this area was the sole producer of glass.

Ill. 3: Piece of rock crystal,
the first "glass" known to man.

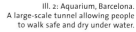

The story goes that one day a (Phoenician) ship belonging to traders in soda called there and spread out along the shore to make a meal. There were no stones on the beach to support their cooking-pots, so they placed lumps of soda from their ship under them. When these became hot and fused with the sand on the beach, streams of an unknown translucent liquid material flowed, and this was the origin of glass".

A stroke of luck, a coincidence, for all three basic ingredients to make glass happened to be there on that beach, quartz (sand), siliciumdioxide; soda, sodium carbonate; and chalk (seashells), calcium carbonate. In the fire these three were fused into siliciumquatrooxide: the basic molecule of glass. (Ill. 4) The clever Phoenician traders soon realized the commercial potential of this shimmering, translucent material, and so glass came into use.

Techniques were developed to manipulate this material, the most intelligent one being the blowpipe. Who would have considered putting a hollow pipe in the hot melt and blow a glass bubble? Someone, reportedly from Syria, had this idea in the first century. It opened up an immense array of possibilities: bottles, cups, vases, ornaments could now be made from glass. (Ill. 5) Further elaborations were worked out leading to beautiful pieces of art like the Diatrata glasses. (Ill. 6)

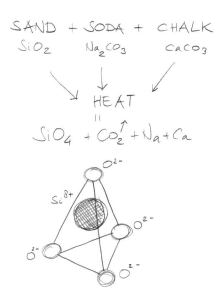

Ill. 4: The basic molecule of glass: SiO4. Notice the negative outside of the pyramid. It is responsible for the little gaps in the material allowing light (photons) to pass but also responsible for the quick cracking of glass.

Ill. 5.2: Through the blowpipe a large bubble is blown and stretched with pincers in the bottle-shape.

Ill. 5.3: The proud craftsman shows the finished bottle.

Ill. 5.1: In a workshop on the island Murano, close to Venice, a part of molten glass is taken out of the furnace using the blowpipe as a tool.

Ill. 6: A Roman glass made in the Diatrata technique. Represented is the Thracian king Lycurgus strangled to death by ivy after insulting Dionysus, the God of wine.

A combination of differently coloured pieces of glass poured over each other and carved out in a cunning way produced these amazing Roman objects of art. Another result of the blowpipe technique was that it was now possible to make glass panels. By blowing a bubble as large as possible, then pricking it open and hence rotating the blowpipe very quickly, a large circular plate of glass was produced. The strongest men were able to produce plates up to a diameter of 1 m. (Ill. 7) This plate could be sliced up in smaller, for instance, rectangular parts, and the window was born. The maximum possible size was limited to about 400 x 300 mm. The pieces of glass which were produced in that way were set in a frame of wood or bronze allowing daylight to enter our living quarters and enabling people inside to look outside without the hindrance of wind, rain or cold.

Ill. 7: After rotating the opened glass bubble a flat circular plate of glass is created.

It is remarkable how architecture reacts to technical improvements. A fairly good example is the shape of windows in houses over the centuries. (Ill. 8) The first windows had to be made from rather small pieces of glass resulting in the well-known medieval window type. The size restrictions came from the production technique: the blowpipe. Also the large beautiful "rose"-windows in Gothic cathedrals were made from this glass. Colours were introduced in the glass by adding certain metal-oxides to the melted glass. Here a lead frame holds the pieces of glass together. Since the lead frame, being rather weak, does not allow a large span, frames made from natural stone had to ensure the structural stability of these windows, which sometimes measured up to 8 m in diameter.

The first technical improvement leading to a change in architecture occurred in the area around Strasbourg where in the 14th century the possibility of blowing not only a sphere but also a cylinder was discovered. When this cylinder was cut open, then heated again and struck flat, larger planes of glass were obtained. At the beginning sizes were only slightly larger than those produced with the rotating blowpipe. However, in around 1750 this cylinder method was improved to possible sizes of 1000 x 800 mm. (Ill. 9) Glass was in those days an expensive material. Production was limited in quantity, and good transparent glass, made from iron-free sand (Bohemia), was extra-

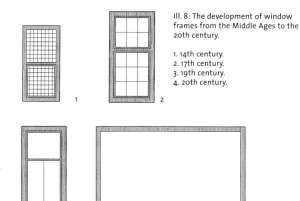

Ill. 8: The development of window frames from the Middle Ages to the 20th century.

1. 14th century.
2. 17th century.
3. 19th century.
4. 20th century.

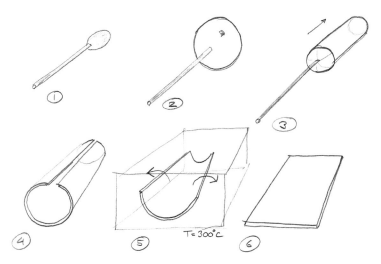

Ill. 9: The method of producing cylinder-blown glass panels.

Ill. 10: Cinderella fits the glass shoe.

expensive. This luxurious aspect is also clear in the role glass plays in fairy-tales. The glass shoes Cinderella wears when the Good Fairy dressed her up is a good example. (Ill. 10) And remember also the glass coffin in which the (very rich) dwarves bury the intoxicated Snow White. The effect of the larger sizes made possible by the cylinder method of glass-panel production on the architecture of windows is evident. (Ill. 11) The next step forward in the technology of glass production came around 1900 when in Belgium the industrial process of pulling of glass was developed. In this process a steel bar is lowered in a pool of molten glass and pulled up slowly. When the steel bar emerges from the molten glass a thin sheet of viscous glass follows the steel bar and the cooling effect of the air solidifies the glass. (Ill. 12) In this way it is possible to produce wide plates of, theoretically, unlimited lengths. The effect was dramatic; large windows opened up buildings in the newly built towns following the development of the increasingly industrialized western world. The latest improvement in glass technology was made in England in the mid-fifties of the 20th century. The name of the process is float glass, indicating the method of production: floating/pouring still liquid glass on a bed of molten tin. Thus the producers were able to make a glass panel with two perfectly flush surfaces, one resulting from the perfectly flat surface of the molten tin, the other, upper one, from gravity that flattened the surface of the molten glass.

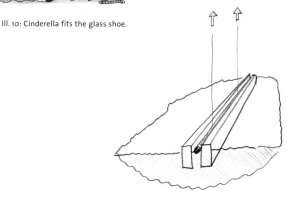

Ill. 12: The process of producing "pulled" glass.

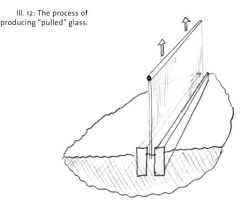

III. 11: Medieval window and 19th-century window in Leiden.

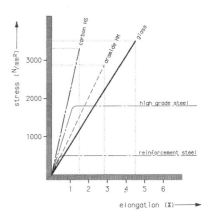

III. 14: This graph shows the potential bearing capacity of laboratory-produced glass compared to other structural materials.

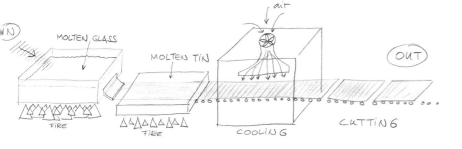

III. 13: The process of producing "float" glass.

III. 16: Curious boys examining the world under a glass panel in the floor of a clubhouse in Arnhem.

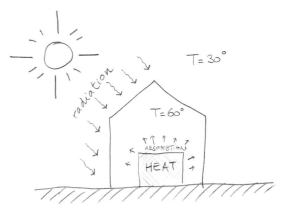

III. 17: Green house effect of an all glass building. Technology and clever design have to solve this uncomfortable effect.

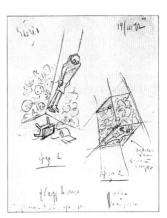

III. 15: Drawing of Sergei Eisenstein for the scenario of the film "Glass House" (1947), showing the psychological effects of living in an all-glass house.

By cooling the slowly forward-moving sheet of glass the glass solidifies and a basically continuous process of making glass panels is created. (III. 13) The impact of this technical progress on architecture was once again enormous. Complete walls/façades were made of single panels. The prize of glass also dropped dramatically allowing glass to be used on a large scale. The exteriors of buildings erected after 1960, in the wake of global post-war economic growth demonstrate this effect. Almost all glass produced is now float glass. Enormous furnaces, modern Moloch ovens, all over the world produce large quantities of glass in a continuous industrial production. Unfortunately, they produce the least acceptable quality; it is cheaper to replace broken panels by new ones than to improve the quality of production or the strength of the product. Where is a market for glass that hardly breaks? (III. 14)

So we have to work with this product of minor quality whose surface is restricted to a maximum of 3.2 x 6.0 m. And, unfortunately enough, only a limited range of thicknesses is produced. At best we may say this makes the challenge to create safe glass structures more interesting. It should also be mentioned that constructing buildings entirely of glass does not create paradise circumstances. There are important social and physical restrictions to glass architecture. The best illustration of the sociological aspect is put forward by the famous Russian film director Sergei Eisenstein who made a simple but very explicit sketch for a film called "Glass House". It illustrates perfectly that too much openness leads to an overwhelming lack of privacy that can make people desperate. (Ills. 15, 16) Also there is a need to take care of climate control: the physical restriction. It is not without meaning that the word "Greenhouse"-effect describes an unpleasant, unwanted phenomenon. We can make insulated glass panels nowadays which keep the warmth inside in winter. Unfortunately, these panels also keep the heat of the sun inside in summer with a fatal effect on the temperature inside. (III. 17) When designing all-glass buildings these two restrictions, the sociological and the physical, have to be taken into account.

The Issue of Safety

Almost all glass produced now is float glass. It is the starting point for the structural design in glass described in this book. But simply using panels of float glass just as they are is certainly not enough to make safe structures. Glass is strong but breaks easily, one of the contradictory, and also dangerous, properties of this very special material.

To create safe structures it is necessary to make a structure redundant (i. e. capable of carrying after failure of a major part) and not ductile. Ductility means that if a structure is slowly reaching the limits of its carrying capacity it breaks or collapses all of a sudden. A good structure must warn by deformation, i. e. cracking noises or whatever signals that an overload and fatal loss of integrity is imminent. Steel has this "warning" property well built into its characteristic material behaviour. When an overload occurs it deforms considerably, the so-called yielding. (Ill. 18) Since steel is an essential component of reinforced concrete this material also has this "warning" property. Wood squeaks and moans when loads grow too big. Glass, as concrete without reinforcement, does not warn if loads become too big. It deforms, but not obviously enough; and cracking occurs all of a sudden with a fatal loss of coherence. Wise structural engineers do not like this "brittle" behaviour: it is

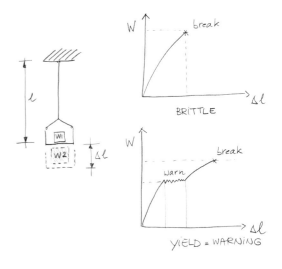

Ill. 18: Building a warning mechanism into the behaviour of the material.

Ill. 19: Exploding Prince Rupert drop directly after the tail has been broken off.

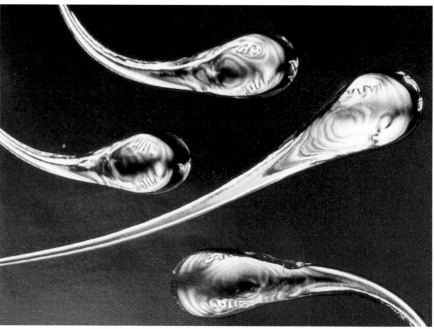

Ill. 20: Intact Prince Rupert drop.

unsafe. Structures must warn before collapsing under an overload and by doing so allow people to flee in time or to take protective measures.

So how do we make safe glass structures that have this "warning" capacity? A single float glass panel breaks all of a sudden under an overload, for instance an impact load of a thrown stone, and falls down in big fragments, the fatal complete loss of integrity. Two essential techniques have been developed to cope with this unwanted property of glass. The first is the toughening of the glass, the second the laminating or layering of glass panels.

The toughening of glass is the artificial introduction of compression in the outside "skin" of a glass panel. This compression closes the existing small cracks that are always present and compensates tensile stresses. Also impact loads are taken far more easily since their tensile peak stress at the impact point is also compensated by the compression in the outside "skin". A very nice illustration of the effect of toughening of glass are the so-called Prince Rupert drops. In 18th-century Bavaria it was found out that if you let glowing drops of molten glass fall into a bucket of water a special type of "glass drop" can be produced. Basically this "drop with a tail" is toughened glass. The water cools quickly the outside, forcing it to set hard while the inside is still hot. It was found out that these drops could be beaten with hammers but would not break. Prince Rupert of Bavaria introduced these drops to the

English court and made them the object of a joke during various dinner parties. Before the party started he told an elegant lady the secret of how to break the drop and at table he challenged strong men to break his drops with a heavy hammer. The proud men had to accept unwillingly the futility of their efforts after furious attempts. When challenged by Prince Rupert the elegant lady broke the drop without any effort causing it to fall apart in a cloud of small glass particles. The trick? She broke the tail and thereby interrupted the balance between the tensile "skin" and the compressed interior. (Ills. 19, 20)

The second improvement to the vulnerability of a single float glass panel is a rather obvious one: if I make two separate beams the structure is safer, for if one beam breaks the other can still carry the load, provided that calculations have been made accurately! This process is called the lamination of glass. An almost invisible foil or glue-layer holds the separate panels together. If you laminate three layers of glass to form one beam you have a safe structure. Even if malicious people start throwing stones from all directions against this poor beam they can only succeed in breaking the two outside layers. Since the foil or glue keeps the broken parts of the two outside panels glued to the central panel these broken parts protect the remaining beam from the stones! If the structural engineer has calculated this central beam accurately for carry-

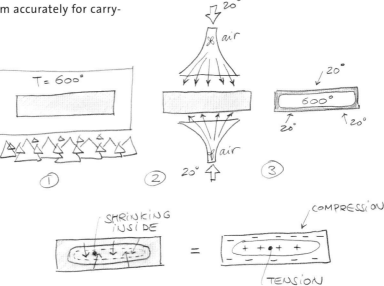

III. 21: Production of toughened glass.

ing normal loads, with a safety factor of 1.1, nothing, besides some extra elastic deformation, will happen. People have time to leave the damaged building, and the owner has time to order a new complete beam and mount it in the place of the damaged one.

It is also possible to laminate toughened glass. With these two techniques we are able to create safe glass structures!

Toughening of Glass

The toughening of glass is a physical progress. One must not forget that the glass as a material is not changed! The glass becomes stronger, less vulnerable but only thanks to the artificial introduction of a compression (stress) in the outside "skin" of the toughened glass element. The procedure of making toughened glass is as follows. A glass panel, complete with all holes and polished edges, is made of normal float glass. In a furnace this element is heated up to about 600 degrees. After taking the panel out of the furnace the outside of the panel is ventilated with air at room temperature. This causes the outside "skin" to cool quickly and hence become hard. The mass of glass on the inside is still very hot and cools down slowly. When a material cools down it inevitably has to shrink. The outside, however, already has its final permanent form. Thus the shrinking part inside, firmly attached to the outside "skin", starts to pull at the hardened outside. This causes compression in the outside "skin" and subsequently, due to balance, tensile stresses in the interior. (III. 21) The effect of the compression in the outside "skin" has the following consequences. Existing scratches and cracks are pushed closed. New scratches undergo the same effect. This means that in a part of the glass structure where the loading on the element leads to tensile stresses the existing cracks cannot open, grow and cause the collapse. Crack growth is a dangerous phenomenon indeed for glass. Glass has no mechanism in its molecular build-up to stop growing cracks. It is just the opposite: a growing crack driven by a tensile stress in the material grows at great speed till it meets a free edge. This brittle behavior is a bad property of glass of which we should always be aware.

Another effect is that the tensile stress, due to loading, first has to "eat up" the compression caused by the toughening. So if toughening has put a compression stress of 100 N/mm^2 in the outside "skin" a tensile stress due to loading of 50 N/mm^2 only leads to a resulting compression of 50 N/mm^2. Normal float glass breaks at about 45 N/mm^2 of tensile stress. So the loading in this example has to produce a tensile stress of 145 N/mm^2 to break this part of toughened glass. This makes it look like the glass has grown in strength from 45 to 145 N/mm^2 but in fact it is only the adding up of the compression due to the toughening process. The glass itself is not changed!

A special effect of the toughening is the pattern of breaking. Float glass breaks into big parts with very sharp edges. Once toughened glass breaks because stress levels exceed the allowable level the complete balance in the toughened glass between the outside, compressed, "skin" and the inside, tensile, part is broken. This leads at once to an exploding release of stresses causing the panel to break into hundreds of small fragments. The effect is well known from the windscreens of older cars which became white screens blocking the view of the driver when hit by a little stone. For this reason, now semi-toughened or strengthened glass is used for windshields. In this type only a small compression stress level is put in the glass using the same method as with normal toughening.

Lamination of Glass

A way to make glass safer is by making not one panel but by gluing, for instance, three panels together. This is a relevant solution because, if a thrown stone hits one single panel, the panel will break inevitably. Also if somewhere in the material the allowable tensile stress is exceeded a single crack will start to grow right away. It will continue to grow from one end of the material to the other since there is no mechanism in glass stopping the crack. In steel for instance the crack will stop against the border of a crystal grid and in concrete the crack will stop against a piece of gravel or a reinforcement bar. In glass the crack will keep on growing and cause complete loss of coherence and thus collapse. If however this broken panel is glued to another one it will remain glued to the unbroken one. Nothing falls down provided that the remaining panel is strong enough to carry the dead load of two panels. A secondary effect is that the broken panel protects the remaining panel from stones thrown from that side. So if we make three panels glued together the central one is protected from all sides. We call the outside panels therefore "sacrificial" panels. If the laminated glass panel is a floor the top sacrificial one is also the panel which takes up wear from daily use (shoes plus dirt). If we make this top layer easily removable we can change this layer every two years and keep the glass as transparent as possible. The principle is clear, but how can two layers of glass be glued together without the joint becoming visible? Two technical solutions have been worked out. The one mostly used is laminating by a transparent foil, called pvb, an abbreviation of the chemical name polyvinylbutyrate. This foil has to be placed on one layer after which the other panel is pressed in a mechanical, evenly distributed manner in a furnace heated up to about 250 degrees. If done correctly, the foil will indeed be invisible. (Ill. 22) However, the measurements of the furnace also limit the possibilities of sizes for laminated panels; in general the largest possible size is 2.50 x 4.50 m. The other way to laminate glass is by resin. In a two-component mixed solution the intermediate joint is filled. The joint hardens out directly after the application of the resin.

Ill. 23: Pyramide Inversée in the Louvre, Paris. A mystifying structure in which steel dominates despite the intention to create a glass pyramid.

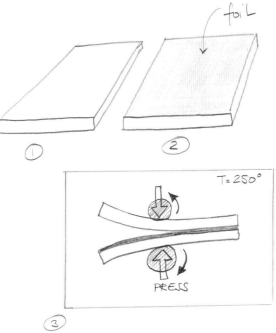

Ill. 22: Production of laminated glass.

Ill. 24, 25: Top view and view from inside of the glass roof in Leiden (Architect: Trude Hooykaaas Ontwerpgroep and Joost Ruland). Although great effort has been made to keep the steel parts as small as possible they play a dominant role.

Slowly we transform each element of a structure into one made entirely of glass: walls, roofs, floors, and columns – no longer delicate, high-tech steel corsets but the abstract, mysterious beauty of pure glass structures. Although steel elements are minimal they still block the view and distract the attention. (Ills. 23 – 25) We will work out all-glass structures with the least

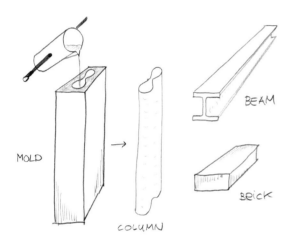

Ill. 28: Survey of possibilities of structural glass elements produced by pouring glass in moulds.

Ill. 26: Testing a glass structure in a Delft Laboratory.

possible amount of other material. For this purpose we must use laboratory tests, preferably on a one-to-one scale, and thus design with the greatest possible safety. (Ill. 26) In fact, we copy the same strategy as was used during the construction of the first big-scale glass and iron building: the Crystal Palace in London.

During construction each iron bar was tested on site with a load three times higher than that which could occur in reality. The bars that passed these tests were safe. This entails the destruction of elements, but, as the German philosopher Friedrich Nietzsche said, you have to destroy something you love in order to understand it. (Ill. 27)

We conducted studies on new methods of working with and manipulating glass. For instance, gluing seems a possible way to make connections between separate elements. Also we must realize that the formability of glass when still molten promises great opportunities. At the moment, this method is applied only when producing objects of art, but possibilities like pouring massive columns and beams or even making glass "bricks" have become thinkable. (Ill. 28)

In this book we describe the first steps in turning glass into a safe and certainly beautiful structural material.

Ill. 27: Broken bar after failure test. Even broken glass remains beautiful.

GLASS BEAMS

The Bridge

"Steady under strain and strong through tension,
Its feet on both sides but in either camp,
It stands its ground, a span of pure attention.
A holding action, the arches and the ramp,
Steady under strain and strong through tension."

Seamus Heaney
(in: "Electric Light", 2001)

Glass bridge in Maastricht, a copy on request
of the original Rotterdam bridge.

Glass Pavilion for the Sonsbeek Art Exhibition
Arnhem, The Netherlands, 1986

Glass Roof for the European Patent Office
Leidschendam, The Netherlands, 1990 – 1991

Glass Roof for a Renovated Office Building
Budapest, Hungary, 1992 – 1994

Glass Footbridges
Rotterdam 1993 – 1994,
Arnhem 1996 and 1999 – 2000,
The Netherlands

Large Glass Beam
Amstelveen, The Netherlands, 1994 – 2000

Glass Stairway for a Museum
Zwolle, The Netherlands, 1995 – 1998

Canopies
Nijmegen, The Netherlands, 1997 – 1999

Finite element calculation image of a
glass beam with a post-tensioning
cable. Study for the Budapest project.

Glass Bridge for Floriade 2002
Hoofddorp, The Netherlands, 1999 – 2002

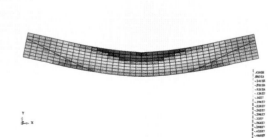

Glass for windows and even floors has been used for ages, although in small measurements. Glass beams, however, are one essential step ahead from the early days of the Roman Empire. The idea for a glass beam is in itself very tempting but also dangerous: if glass breaks, it breaks completely, because the cohesion is lost. An overload or a stone thrown at it results in a total, and also sudden, failure of the beam. This is unacceptable, also because we like to have a warning mechanism in our structures that is activated when things get too demanding. A steel beam, for instance, warns by large deformation and the so-called yielding, a plastic deformation.

Glass in itself has no such "warning" property. It is only the invisible gluing together of individual panes, a process called laminating, which enables us to make a safe beam. Laminating of glass was invented in the early 1900s when – so the story goes – a scientist dropped by accident a glass bottle containing glue and as a result found on the floor, a few days later, two glass fragments glued together invisibly. In the evening paper of that same day he read about a girl who died in a car injured by a broken windshield which smashed when hit by a gravel grain. He realized that if the windshield had been built of two layers of glass, glued together invisibly, this tragic accident might not have happened. This idea was an initial impulse for the industrial production of laminated glass. Another major impulse came when the chemical firm DuPont de Nemours invented a transparent foil called pvb (polyvinyl-butyrate), which glues glass panes to each other. Production takes place in an autoclave under pressure at a temperature level of about 250°C. The glass panes and the foils or plies are rolled together under considerable pressure. The result is a perfect transparent piece of glass composed of two, or even up to ten, individual panes of glass. In this way safe glass beams are produced not by making one beam but by gluing two or more beams together. If a malignant person throws a stone at your precious glass beam he can only break the outside panes. These broken panes keep on sticking to the central ones and thus protect them.

For these reasons the concept of a glass beam was "in the air" in the 1980s. Various members of the international community of structural engineers carried out studies. But who would dare to put the first glass beam in a real building? The psychological barrier was enormous, for we know from everyday practice that glass breaks easily. Clients and contractors have a tendency to avoid risky experiments. The building industry is one of the most conservative industries. Thus new technologies are being critically watched, and questions are being asked in order to make completely sure about the material's behaviour, not only during construction but also during long-term normal use.

New developments need an enthusiastic client willing to take a certain risk. The engineer naturally has to assume the obligation to analyze all possibilities of unwelcome effects of the proposed innovation. The introduction of glass beams is a good example of a hesitantly accepted innovation.

Test on glass bar round 30 mm to measure the ultimate tensile bending stress. A series of tests was carried out to determine the statistically acceptable value for this special type of glass.

Glass Pavilion for the Sonsbeek Art Exhibition

Arnhem, The Netherlands, 1986

"A One-Summer Wonder"

Every five years or so a large art exhibition is held in Arnhem in a former estate, now a city park, called Sonsbeek. For this event modern art is arranged at various places in the park itself and in the stately mansion on top of a hill. Temporary pavilions to exhibit objects of art had been erected for former events by well-known Dutch architects such as Gerrit Rietveld and Aldo van Eyck. Rietveld's pavilion was later moved to the Kröller Müller Museum in the Hoge Veluwe National Park (NL) for permanent use.

Connection detail: column, façade panels and steel roof truss.

The original idea was a tunnel of glass, housing vulnerable objects of art. At a later stage a small steel truss was added to span the roof. The main portal frame is formed by two disc-shaped glass columns, depth 580 mm, height 3,650 mm (toughened glass t = 15 mm) bolted to a concrete foundation slab. The transfer of forces uses the friction forces created by the clamping of the bolts. It is therefore essential that a 3-mm-thick neoprene sheet is placed in the contact plane between the glass of the column and the steel angles bolted to the concrete foundation.

For the 1986 exhibition a team of two young architects, Jan Benthem and Mels Crouwel, was asked to design a pavilion as an accommodation for the more vulnerable objects of art. They came up with the project of a glass tunnel leading from a path at the foot of the hill to the old mansion. Through this tunnel the visitors could walk to the villa while enjoying the view of the majestic old trees of the surrounding park together with the intriguing presence of modern art.

ABT was asked to do the structural engineering of this special pavilion. The consulting engineer in charge was Michel van Maarschalkerwaart, a gifted man. While working out together the initial ideas of the architects, they made clear that the walls and the roof should be as transparent as possible, with the exception that the beam carrying the roof should be a fragile

Side view, with faint shadow
thrown on the grass.

steel truss so that the building would not be too invisible. Hans Christian
Andersen's fairy-tale of the Emperor's Clothes was mentioned in relation to this
"invisibility"; there had to be something of a real building on site. Since this
was a temporary pavilion, the strict building codes and standards fortunately
would only have to be implemented in part. The design we worked out with the
architects was simple: glass fins of the type used in the 1950 car showrooms
acted as columns, the roof beam was a truss consisting of slender steel angles
and thin bar-type diagonals. The roof and the walls consisted of laminated glass
panels of a considerable size. The joints were silicone, the floor consisted of
wood-chips. That was all.

Transversal stability was achieved by the frame action of the two
glass columns, each clamped firmly in a concrete foundation block, combined

**The steel truss spanning the roof connects the two columns. The span of the truss
is 6.20 m, the depth 600 mm. The connection between the steel
truss and the glass column is by clamping. In this way the portal
frame is stable in a transversal direction; it can absorb horizontal
forces in the direction of the plane of the portal frame.**

Side elevation, almost completely transparent.

with the steel truss carrying the roof. Longitudinal stability was created by the
in-plane stiffness of the glass panels in the façades. The steel truss was connected to the glass columns by clamping the steel angles to the glass surface with
a neoprene pad in between. Basically, this was a structurally straightforward
pavilion the beauty of which consisted partly in achieving a mysterious presence
in the natural surroundings. Shining in the sunlight and reflecting the scenery it
told about the wonderful possibilities of glass structures. One of the lessons of
the Sonsbeek Pavilion was that glass is transparent but not invisible. It reflects
the surroundings in a very visible way, deforms reality by a diversion of the light
and even casts a vague shadow (5 % of the light is caught in the glass).

But first we had to convince the authorities in charge of a few
basic starting-points, such as the simple method we had chosen to provide

longitudinal stability by the in-plane stiffness of the façade. For this one needs to transfer a small quantity of shear force through the silicone joints. Taking into account, as a standard, the storms which statistically take place every fifty years, we calculated this shear stress convoked by the shear force to be 0.10 N/mm^2. However, at first no stress at all was allowed in the joints by the authorities. They asked us whether we were able to predict how the silicone would behave after having been exposed to the severe Dutch polar winter (in April) and (four months later) to the tropical Dutch summer? The supplier of the silicone povided us with long-duration climate tests performed in the USA, which proved that shear stress of up to 0.14 n/mm^2 was acceptable. Eventually, we were given the benefit of the doubt, especially when we presented a big aquarium consisting entirely of glass panels and silicone joints – a type that can be found in the living room

Inside view, detail of the connection of steel truss and glass column.

The glass walls stand on little Perspex blocks on concrete foundation slabs. They are directly connected by a silicone joint to the columns and the glass roof slabs. The glass wall provides stability in longitudinal direction. It consists of a series of big plates (annealed glass t = 10 mm, measuring 2.00 x 3.65 m) connected by a silicone joint which takes up the shear stresses provoked by the action of longitudinal wind.

The roof consists of a laminated glass panel (2 x 10 mm annealed glass glued together by a polyvinylbutyral (pvb) foil). These panels rest on the steel trusses, which are, to this end, provided with two steel angles to form a support.

of many Dutch households. And if Dutch households accept the risk of shear stress up to 3 N/mm^2 – which occurs in these "structures" – then why should 0.10 N/mm^2, a level reached only during the worst possible statistical storm within 50 years, not be acceptable to the municipality? Our argument was gracefully accepted.

In another field we had to yield to the demand for the foundations to be set in the ground at a frost-free level. This meant that foundations were required to be 700 mm deep in the ground, which led to a loss of free height in the pavilion of 500 mm because the height of the glass columns was limited (then) to 3.5 m due to workshop limitations. The argument was that the destiny of the Rietveld Pavilion indicated that temporary pavilions might become permanent installations. We had to accept that they were right, theoretically.

When in October 1986 the pavilion in the Sonsbeek Park was dismantled there were rumours that it would be bought by a zoo to provide a presumably safe walk through a lion-pit. Reality was less romantic though; the glass was recycled like all glass elements which are no longer in use. Glass is, after all, the most recycled material in the world.

View through the pavilion; lines and shadows mark the presence of the building.

As the pavilion was built against a hill in Sonsbeek Park, ventilation could take place through the steel trusses. Thus the decision in favour of steel trusses led to an avoidance of the greenhouse effect during hot summer days.

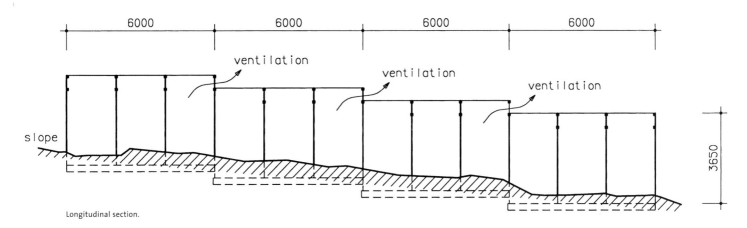

Longitudinal section.

Cross section.

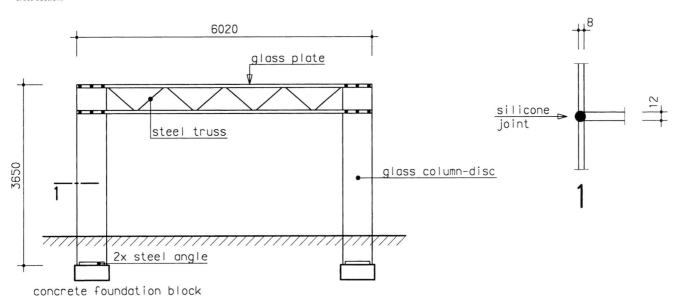

Glass Roof for the European Patent Office

Leidschendam, The Netherlands, 1990 – 1991

"Shattered Dreams, Wrong Bet"

The success of the Sonsbeek pavilion drew a lot of attention. For me personally it was the start of a sincere interest in glass used structurally. Further enquiry into the material confirmed that glass was a promising, structurally reliable material. At the same time, the wish to make open and transparent buildings as an expression of the zeitgeist manifested itself more and more clearly in the world of architecture.

Two young Dutch architects won a prestigious international competition for the European Patent Office. The brief called for a representative building

Model. Each garden has its individual design theme by landscape architect Yves Brunier. In front the three central buildings: restaurant (cone), congress hall (sphere) and library (inverted cone).

The glass structures are part of the roofs between the office building and the three big building volumes for the central facilities. They are glass boxes, placed on top of the steel beams which span the 20 m distance between the central facilities and the offices. Each box has two parallel glass sidewalls, which, like beams, span the distance of about 9 m between the steel beams.

The glass beams are laminated by 3 panes of 8 mm toughened glass. Normally, this kind of glass is limited to a length of 4.50 m. By laminating with resin instead of pvb-foils and by using alternating joints – so that two panels are continuous when one is stopped – a continuous beam spanning 9 m could be made. The glass beams are tapered, measuring 2.50 m at the highest point.

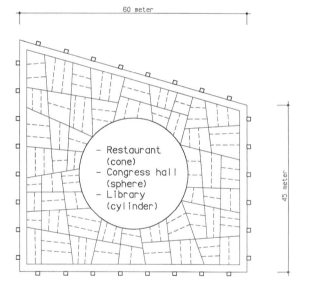

Pattern of steel beams.

comprising about 200,000 m² of office space, for some 1,500 highly trained patent-examiners plus a large staff. The winning design by Willem Jan Neutelings and Frank Roodbeen was both simple and brilliant. An asymmetrical grid of rooms in three stories created high-class offices overlooking beautiful theme-based gardens. In front of the main building three larger volumes of elementary shape were planned: a steel/glass cone housing the restaurant, a concrete sphere containing the conference rooms and a tapered wooden cylinder for the library or study-center.

A glass roof, parts of it spanning up to 25 m, covered the spaces around these three volumes, connecting them to the office structure. This was the opportunity to create a spectacular glass structure with ambitious architects, an ample budget and a head full of structural ideas as optimal starting condi-

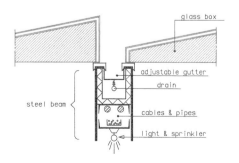

Cross section of steel beam integrating various functions.

tions. So the team developed the "glass box" concept, aiming at an easily

mountable structure of insulated glass made from workshop elements. In the

context of this big project it was possible to conduct additional studies concern-

ing the possibilities of structural glass. Contacts with glass manufacturers and

other professionals working with glass became much easier because of the

promise of a large order.

The exciting question at the end of the final design phase was

whether we would be able to stay within the budget and combine all special

wishes and the ensuing costs. We were – but then almost out of the blue came

the announcement that the member states of the Patent Office organisation

would postpone the project. The Dutch government, we were told, thought it

wise to give up this building, in exchange for the more prestigious European

**To avoid tensile forces in the glass the centre glass panel was recessed and in this
recess a pre-tensioned steel cable was attached. Insulated glass
panels were placed in between and on top of the glass beams,
attached to the beams and to each other by steel connection
details. The intention was to assemble a complete box on the
ground and lift it directly on top of the steel beams.**

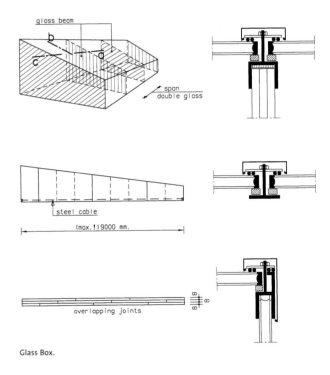

Glass Box.

Details of glass boxes.

Bank – which in the end turned out to be a wrong bet. But as an outcome, it

was through the impetus of publishing and presenting papers about the

structural possibilities of glass that activities for this project started to draw

attention.

Glass Roof for a Renovated Office Building

Budapest, Hungary, 1992 – 1994

"The Contemplating Whale Floating in a Sea of Glass"

When the Berlin Wall came down in November 1989 this, among many more important effects, paved the way for capitalist entrepreneurship in the eastern part of Europe. One of the new markets was the insurance and banking business. For the Dutch firm "Nationale Nederlanden ING Bank" came a golden opportunity to start up a new organisation in Budapest and venture onto the Eastern European market. For this purpose they bought a large, stately neo-classical building in one of the most prestigious streets of Budapest, the Andrássy út. Once a wealthy residence for well-to-do families situated around an

Glass roof and floating object on top of the stately 19th-century structure.

Glass beams span the distance of about 4.50 m between the main HEB 360 steel beams. Each glass beam consists of 3 layers, laminated by pvb-foils: two 8 mm panels on the outside for protection and extra safety, and one 12 mm layer as the actual structural beam.
Float glass was used for the outside panels because it breaks up into big parts, thus protecting the inner structural plate more efficiently. Scratches and free-flowing water would not be able to reach the surface of the structural plate and the two outer plates would take up all inflicted damage. The depth of a glass beam is 400 mm; the centre-to-centre distance of the beams is 1 m. The insulated glass panels forming the roof are laid directly on the glass beams and connected to the beams with an internal bolted detail to take up uplift forces due to the wind.

inner courtyard, this chic, stylish building had been reduced by the Communist regime to a semi-ruin. The roof had rotted away and in the impressive façade an alarming decay had set in. The local authorities committed ING Vastgoed, in charge of the new property development for the owner, to restore the façade to its original state; inside there were no restrictions. A new roof with an extra floor was possible, too, but the modern facilities had to be hidden from the people in the streets. ING Vastgoed invited the young Dutch architectural firm Mecanoo to restore the outside of the building whilst at the same time displaying the modern age to visitors to the inside by dazzling them with the latest design features from Western Europe.

At a first meeting in the Delft office of Mecanoo, the architects, a team led by Erick van Egeraat, explained their intention. They wanted to remove

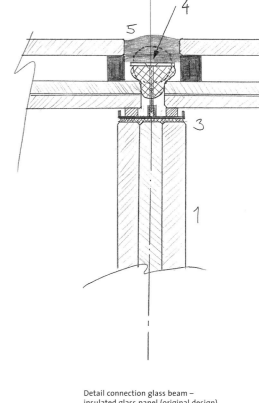

Detail connection glass beam – insulated glass panel (original design).

1. Glass beam.
2. Insulated glass panel.
3. Aluminium strip glued to top of glass beam (little gutter).
4. Soft neoprene bar; compressed during assembling (second line of defence).
5. Silicone joint (first line of defence).

the rotten roof, insert a new restaurant floor and top it all off with a maximum transparency roof, i.e. a glass roof.

The basic idea was that standing on a firm concrete floor and looking up people would see a discrete, discontinuous layer of steel beams, a shimmering plane of insulated glass and then the clouds.

The span from wall to wall was about 20 m, but a few columns could be placed in the restaurant providing extra support for the ribs (= beams) of the roof. These steel beams pinned down a strangely shaped "body", which the design team readily named "the whale". This whale housed two conference rooms on two levels: one room looking into the former open courtyard now covered with the glass roof, the other presenting a beautiful view over the roofs of Budapest.

Executed detail of "floating" joint. The mechanical connection is placed in the cavity; a silicone joint provides extra water tightness.

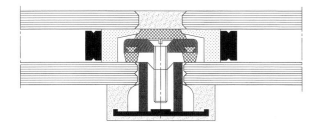

View over the glass roof to the city of (Buda) Pest. The glass-clad building on the right houses the building services.

The main steel beams were placed at a distance of about 4 m from centre-to-centre; the spans, however, were not straight but more or less tapered. From our experience with the European Patent Office we could confirm the architects' eager enquiry that it was possible to use glass beams for the secondary span between steel beams. A lot of research went into the connection between the glass beams and the insulated glass panels put on top of them, which had to be as small as possible (= invisible). The first detail was based on the concept of the continuous neoprene tube sealed with a silicone joint. It got its final shape later, when Portal, a Belgian firm who got the contract for this roof, imparted their knowledge. This detail had two lines of defence against leakage, the first being the silicone joint, the second a little internal gutter on top of the glass beam, ending in the real gutter. The structural connection was finally constructed with small screws clamping the glass panels to the glass beam and a continuous aluminium strip glued onto the top of the glass beam. Although this looks frail the uplifting force of the wind is only small, due to the dead load of the glass panels resulting in small stresses in the glued aluminium-to-glass connection. This detail proved to work very well, for during the mounting of the roof the water tightness was secured for almost half a year by nothing but the little gutter. Silicone could not be used, for the outside temperature was below 5°C.

Then the architects enquired whether it would be possible to put the secondary glass beams on little columns, hence lift up the whole roof and create an even more surprising effect. Now the whole roof area can be considered as forming one plate. Two sides were already firmly attached to the massive

View through the edge of the glass roof. Thermal bridges were of no concern in the Budapest that had just emerged from behind the Iron Curtain.

To emphasize the transparency/lightness of the roof each glass beam is placed on two small stainless steel columns, massive bars round 30 mm. The stability of the roof floor with the lifted beams is provided for by attaching the horizontal plane of the roof to two walls of the building and by two bracings of steel bars in the façade.

1-m spans between the glass beams give the space its rhythm.
The undersides of the glass beams show as black lines.

Inside view of the water proofing detail in the connection of glass beam to insulated glass panels.

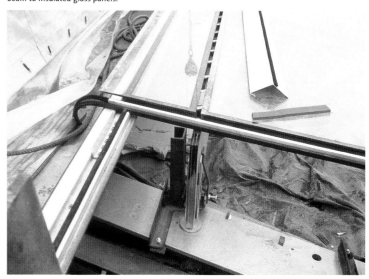

Plan of glass roof. To the right the
building services roof structure. At
the bottom large windows in the
oblique tile-clad roof.

Three models for testing the
connection of steel column to glass
beam.

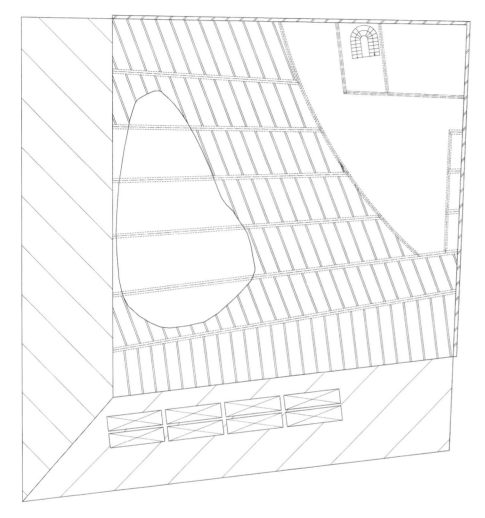

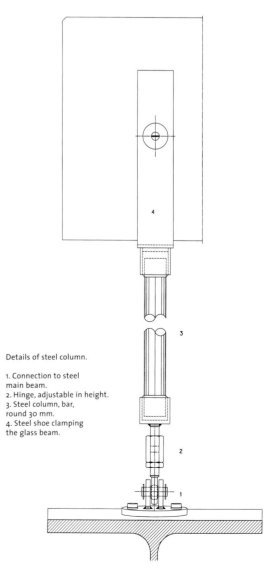

walls. So we only had to supply anchoring steel ties in a few places to stabilize

this uplifted roof-plane. Hence we could put the roof on little columns and in

doing so also create the slope needed for the rainwater drainage. We opted for

a 5° slope, which makes the raindrops flow smoothly into the gutter and leave

no dirt or stains caused by pools of water drying up. We even studied little glass

columns instead of the steel ones. But that proved to be a little too innovative.

So, amid this glass ocean the whale, with the skeleton made of

laminated wood and clad with a skin of zinc, floats quietly and seems to contem-

plate its wondrous presence in Budapest because somewhere a wall dividing a

city crumbled under its own social weight.

Details of steel column.

1. Connection to steel
main beam.
2. Hinge, adjustable in height.
3. Steel column, bar,
round 30 mm.
4. Steel shoe clamping
the glass beam.

Glass Footbridges

Rotterdam 1993 – 1994, Arnhem 1996 and 1999 – 2000, The Netherlands

Rotterdam: "Walk through the Air with Your Shadow on the Ground"

Rotterdam-based architect Dirk Jan Postel was facing a curious problem. The growing architectural firm of which he was one of the directors was housed in a renovated pumping station. The first floor of an adjacent building they were able to rent brought up the question of how to avoid having to go outdoors to the other office. It would be nice to have a little bridge spanning the 3.5 m gap, but then the architecture of the 1950s buildings was so sober and so characteristic that any bridge would look out of place. Except if it was a transparent one. The architect remembered to have recently read something

Cross section of the connection detail of
glass beam, glass floor and glass wall.

1. Glass beam.
2. Glass floor.
3. Stainless steel cable connecting
the wall to the suspended floor.
4. Exterior stainless steel end plate
attached to cable.
5. Glass wall.

The glass bridge is basically composed of two parts: the load-carrying part formed by two beams and the floor plates, and the part which gives protection from wind and rain, consisting of two walls and a roof. The carrying beams span about 3.50 m and have a depth of 300 mm. The underside of each beam is polished in a rounded shape for architectural reasons. The composition of the glass beam is 3 x 10 mm float glass. Different from the Budapest glass beams for extra bearing capacity in normal conditions, the two protective outside layers were made as thick as the inner structural layer. The glass panels are 2 x 15 mm float glass glued on top of the glass beams by an adhesive silicone strip.

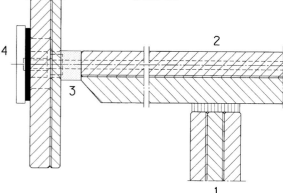

right:
View of the transparent floor
on the way to the other side.

below:
Two connection details: steel shoe
holding and stabilizing the glass
beam, small cantilevering
steel arm holding the glass wall.

about glass beams. That was the time when the progress of the Budapest project spread through the architectural offices like a wildfire. Dirk Jan contacted me to discuss possibilities.

Very quickly the outlines were drawn. We split the bridge up into two parts: a structural part, carrying the people crossing, composed of two glass beams and a glass plate on top of them, and a glass "raincoat" (= walls + roof) offering protection against the rain and wind.

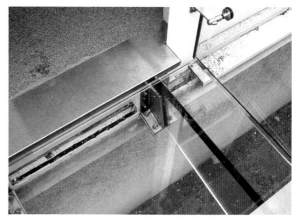

Architecture in an all-glass structure is entirely a matter of details and especially of how to design them. The architect realized that the ideal beam would have a curved bottom. So it was designed. The connecting details were made of stainless steel, a material that is an architecturally perfect match for glass. Still it was a problem to find someone to build it. Alverre, a specialized firm from the town of Almelo in the eastern part of the Netherlands, and its director Ton van der Meulen showed an interest in glass structures. They agreed to realize the structure, but the architect, like the client, would have to take a certain part of the risk.

One sunny day in April 1994 it was completed: The Glass Bridge. Weird it was and frightening to walk through the air some 3 m up. Also the fact that there was no handrail made it scary, although the municipality had us smash a heavy sandbag against the glass wall to prove its safety. Dirk Jan had the courage to opt for a transparent glass floor since this certainly dramatizes the crossing. As the bridge only crosses a hidden one-way alley no female employee objected.

Mounting the glass bridge in May 1994. An anxious Dirk Jan Postel follows the work.

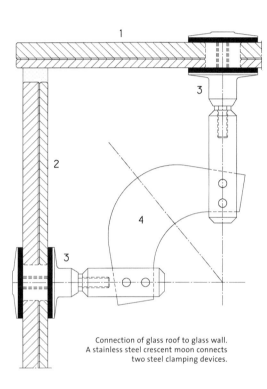

Connection of glass roof to glass wall. A stainless steel crescent moon connects two steel clamping devices.

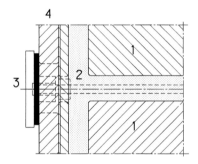

Top view of wall-floor connection.

1. Glass floor panels.
2. Silicone filled joints.
3. Stainless steel cable and end plate.
4. Glass wall.

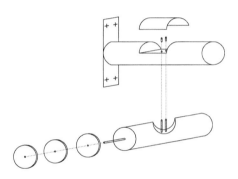

Principle of main detail, which carries the weight of the glass wall and glass roof. (See also illustration of the mounting.)

View from under the bridge. People seem to flow in the air. This image inspired the glass floor in the Educatorium.

The bridge has been used for about eight years now and everything is well. Condensation against the single glass panels occurs only very occasionally, and the drops of water quickly disappear because of the large amount of natural ventilation. Summer and winter differences in movement due to temperature are absorbed by the flexible design of the details. The glass floor panels are not treated in any way; one simply walks over the glass surface. It is not slippery at all and shows only a few scratches since it is a carpet-to-carpet crossing. One morning there was a big stain on the glass wall from a beer bottle smashed against it, but our structure proved to be stronger than bad intentions. One year later a street-tile was thrown, which crashed the first layer. But as was expected, despite having broken into thousands of pieces, the toughened glass panel protected the inner panel. The safety concept worked.

Arnhem: "A Dutch Treat"

Soon after we were asked for another project if such a construction could be made simpler and cheaper. The actual purpose was spanning the gap between an older and a more recent building for the Arnhem Zoo that stood only 3.80 m apart from each other. The architect left out all sophisticated stainless steel details and made simple silicone joints; their ability to transport small stresses was now recognized even by the local authorities. For the connection to the buildings we created what we call the Postman Solution: let the glass panel wall slide into a slit. We even tried to combine the load-carrying beam with the walls, which are of course big "beams" themselves; a logical thought, but this proved to be too much for the production firm. The interesting feature of the roof is that the glass is rounded in order to have a good flow of rainwater.

The laminated walls consist of an outer protective layer of 12 mm toughened float glass and an inner structural layer of 6 mm toughened glass. The roof is made out of one top layer of 8 mm and an inner layer of 12 mm, both float glass. All laminations are done by pvb-foils. All physical connections are made by the silicone joints; no steel details here!

Second Glass Bridge Arnhem: "Double Fun"

This quiet and modest glass bridge is a remarkable feature at the entrance of the Arnhem Zoo.

The bridge proved such a success for the client that a second one was opted for to connect the other side of the building to the adjacent buildings. There was a considerable difference in height between the two buildings which had to be connected. It was decided to make a glass bridge with a stair built into it. Basically, it is simple to cut out the top of the glass beam in the shape of a stair. Modern techniques like laser cutting or high water-pressure cutting enable workshops to cut out any shape. The shape will be cut out by computer from a glass panel in one go. A major advantage of these methods compared to the ordinary hole drilling with steel is that the sidewalls of the hole are quite

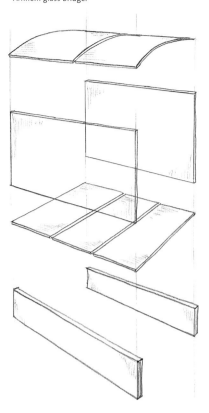

Exploded view of the first Arnhem glass bridge.

First Arnhem glass bridge. Connections are made by the (long) silicone joints instead of steel details.

Underside of the second Arnhem bridge. Note the separated walls and floor/stair structure. The glass is sandblasted to block the view from below.

smooth and thus give less opportunity for cracks. But these methods are rather

expensive, yet. Apart from the discussed difference of shape, the detailing of

the second glass bridge is identical to the first one.

But I am still waiting for the client who asks for a glass bridge

200 m in the air between two skyscrapers. This would really be a psychological

challenge!

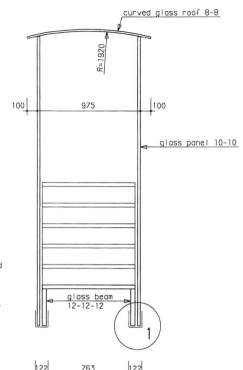

Basic cross section of the second
glass bridge in Arnhem.

1. Glass beams.
2. Translucent glass floor panels.
3. Glass wall panels.
4. Glass roof (curved).

Side view of the second Arnhem
bridge, a combination of a bridge
and a glass stair.

Large Glass Beam

Amstelveen, The Netherlands, 1994 – 2000

"A Glass Beam spanning 26 Meters"

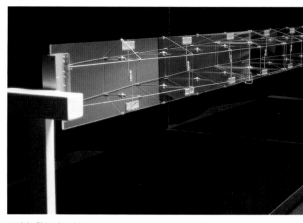

Model of big glass beam.

For the design of the new headquarters of the "Zwitserleven" insurance company, situated at the A9 motorway in Amstelveen, the Architekten Cie. (in this case architect Pi de Bruyn) asked for assistance for three special structures supposed to "innovate" the building: A large glass plane hanging in front of the highway façade helping to reduce the noise (this more or less standard steel/glass façade is not described here); a maximum-transparency restaurant roof (see pages 62 – 65); five large glass beams spanning a courtyard-like recess in the building.

Plans and technical details of big glass beam.

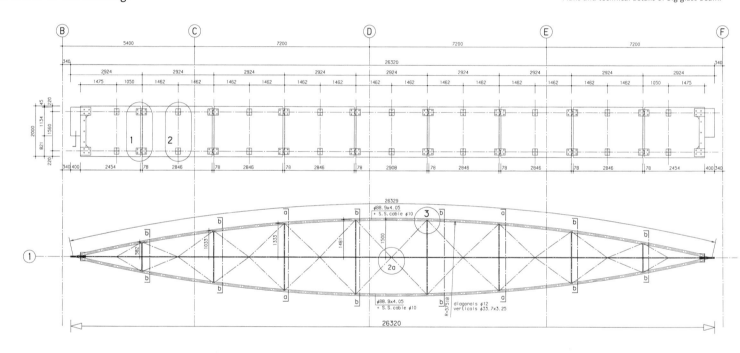

The task of the beams was to suggest in a mysterious way the cubic shape of the original design that had been disturbed by recesses introduced to increase the length of the façade and allow for more windows and offices. The beams were also meant to act like louvres, reducing the impact of sunlight on the façade, but this effect was calculated to be only small and unfortunately did not work that way. Two beams survived as architectural artefacts, but their special feature is that they had to span 26 m.

Due to production and transport limitations in Europe the maximum length of a laminated glass panel is about 4.50 m. In a few cases – if you are willing to wait long and pay much – they can be up to 7 m long. So the problem is how to connect several glass panels structurally. In everyday practice this is done by clamping, with two steel plates and bolts, through

Position of the two glass beams in the plan of the building.

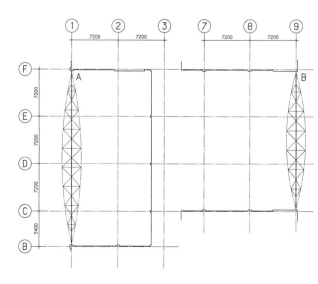

large-diameter holes in the glass. The maximum force is dictated by the
maximum compression force delivered by the bolts and by the friction between
the unavoidable neoprene interlayer and the glass. This technology requires
large steel plates and a lot of bolts, and both certainly do not help to enhance
the image of a glass beam. And then there is also the problem of the wind
pushing and pulling at the upright placed panels of glass. We tackled the wind
problem by making a web of cables and bars around the glass panels, a
structural web that would shimmer around the main element: the Glass Beam.

The problem in connecting steel and glass is the transportation
of forces from the former to the latter. If we just let a bolt in shear force do
the job in direct contact between steel and glass, a big force is locally pushing
against the glass, which will not be able to take up this local stress and will

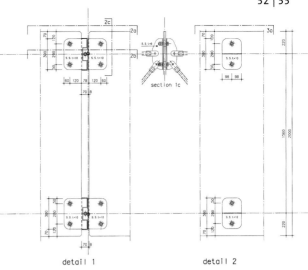

detail 1   detail 2

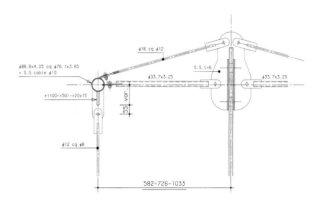

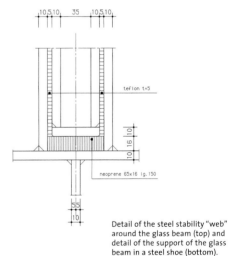

Detail of the steel stability "web"
around the glass beam (top) and
detail of the support of the glass
beam in a steel shoe (bottom).

**Two types of beams were developed, one for a span of 21.60 m and one for a span
of 27.00 m, each consisting of assembled panels. Each panel has 3
layers, two t = 6 mm on the outside and a central one of 15 mm.
All glass is toughened. The measurements of all panels, except the
ones at the supports, are 2,944 x 2,000 mm. The 21.60 m beam is
composed of 7 panels; the 27 m beam has 9 panels.
Steel plates and bolts connect the glass panels. For the transfer of forces through
these connections a special type of detailing was developed.
Instead of transfer by friction, a detail was developed using shear
transfer in the plane of the glass. In this way the force is
transported from the glass to a nylon infill, then to a steel bolt-
axis, further to a steel plate, which crosses the gap between the
two glass panels.**

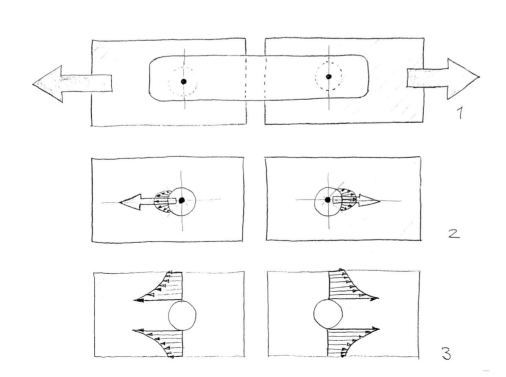

Transfer of tensile forces.

1. The gap/joint between two glass panels is
transferred by two steel strips, each on one side of
the glass.
2. From the steel strip the force is transferred by a bolt
to a nylon plug. The nylon plug is a flexible medium
transporting the force in a "spring-like" way to the
glass panel. Bolt holes can be drilled to fit perfectly.
3. In the glass panel itself the force evokes dangerous
tensile stresses in the section between the hole and
the edge of the panel. At this point, where the stress
has the highest value due to the effect of stress-
concentration, failure will start.

surely crack. Therefore we have to find a way to transport this force in a smooth, slightly "elastic" way from the bolt to the glass. To this purpose we created the following detail:

1.   Drill a big hole in the glass, about five times the diameter of the bolt;

2.   Always let the edges of the hole be polished thoroughly and let the rims be arris edges, in order to avoid stress-concentrations due to little cracks or damages caused by the drilling;

3.   Glue a nylon (polyacetate) or POM (polyoxymethylate) plug in the hole and make sure it is almost the size of the diameter of the hole; the glue is only meant to hold the plug in position and should have the least possible thickness;

In the steel plate a so-called door-hinge detail was incorporated to take up any tolerances. Hence compression and tensile forces resulting from bending moments could be taken up. Also shear forces could be transported in this detail due to the fact that steel can take up large shear forces.

By connecting the 27-mm-thick glass panels a very slender beam is created which, if loaded like that, would buckle out of plane immediately. Therefore a supporting steel structure was worked out which would secure the glass beam against buckling.

Steel shoes attached to the building support the beams and allow them to move according to temperature.

4.   Put the steel plates, and of course the neoprene pads, on the glass and, on site, hence without any variation (!), drill a fitting hole for the steel bolt through the nylon. Thereafter the bolts can be tightened.

If a force starts to pull at the bolt, the shear force will be transported from the bolt to the nylon plug, and because of the low E-Modulus the force from the bolt will be spread out till the nylon pushes against the glass over a large area, hence not creating any stress-peak due to pressure.

This type of connection has another useful feature as well: it is an "elastic" connection, it can take up sudden loads smoothly! This is always a favourable property reducing the vulnerability of the structure. For another project, a museum in Rotterdam (see pages 86 – 87), we had already worked this

Polyamide: PA
Tradenames: Nylon, Ertalon, Nylatron, Sustamid.

Mass	1,140 kg/m³
Tensile stress (ultimate)	50 N/mm²
Strain	> 160 %
Modules	1,500 N/mm²
Bending stress (ultimate)	40 N/mm²
Compression stress (ultimate)	65 N/mm²
Temperature range	- 40 to 100°C
Moisture (at 70° air moisture content)	3 %

Polyoxymethylate: POM
Tradenames: Delrin, Hostaform, Ertacall, Sustarin

Mass	1,410 kg/m³
Tensile stress (ultimate)	65 N/mm²
Strain	> 30 %
Modules	3,000 N/mm²
Bending stress (ultimate)	120 N/mm²
Compression stress (ultimate)	100 N/mm²
Temperature range	- 40 to 100°C
Moisture (at 70° air moisture content)	0.25 %

Note:
– There is a need for UV-protection (steel plates over the plug).
– Keep stresses low to avoid the effect of possible creep.
– It is possible to increase the ultimate stress values by a factor 2 or 3 by adding glass fibre (about 25 % of the weight) to the material.

Laboratory test on the main connection detail in the big glass beam.

out to open up the structural connection. It all sounds perfectly simple and

logical. But life is not like that! Laboratory tests showed the potential of the

method but also revealed an unpleasant side effect when testing to the

ultimate limit: small eccentricities caused the nylon plug to rotate and by doing

so cause failure. Placing a steel plate, a little smaller than the nylon plug, on

both sides of the plug, stopped this phenomenon. However, almost four years

after the presentation of this concept we were still discussing and writing

letters to lawyers to get the contractor to build it like we wanted it to be built.

The contractor was quick to make an alternative proposal to the client: a steel

structure with a glass-panel cladding. The client and the architect refused. The

contractor did not want to build the glass louvres, the name we gave to these

glass beams, considering the concept to be unsafe and dangerous, although I

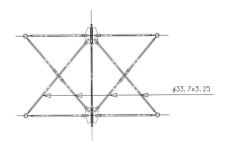

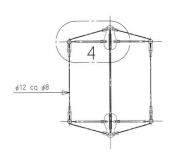

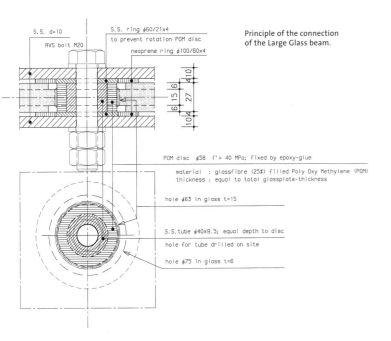

Principle of the connection
of the Large Glass beam.

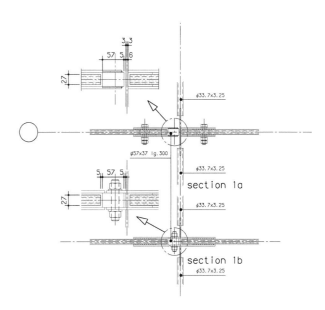

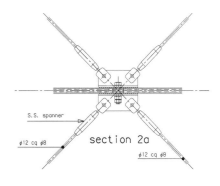

wonder whether this point of view is dictated by sheer beneficial interest in

the public or by a simple financial calculation. But who am I to say so, having

an emotional relationship with the original, unique louvre structure? In 2000

they axed the glass beam. A glittering minimized stainless steel tube with

suspension cables now closes the cubic shape of the building. But a lot of

valuable knowledge had resulted from this experience.

Details and elements of the structure
for the Large Glass Beam.

Glass Stairway for a Museum

Zwolle, The Netherlands, 1995 – 1998

"Walking on (Thin) Ice"

Zwolle is a modest-size town in the eastern part of the Netherlands on the banks of the river Ijssel. It has a rich history and once was part of the medieval commercial chain of cities called the Hanse. To display archaeological objects and also to exhibit historical and modern art a few blocks of houses in the town centre were bought to be combined into a City Museum. One part of the ensemble would be demolished and transformed into the new entrance hall. The Zwolle-based architect Gerard van der Belt won the competition for the design of the new museum. In his design the new hall was the central element,

Basic elements of the stair during construction. Two glass banisters act as big beams. The glass treads rest glued onto glass brackets.

This stairway is composed of two flights of stairs, which share a platform halfway in the air. Since the glass beams, which form the banisters, are about 11 m long they had to be composed of several panels. Each panel is 3 x 10 mm laminated, annealed glass. The connections of the glass panels are basically worked in the same detailing as at the Zwitserleven beam (see pages 32 – 35), but instead of the hinged centre part we combined the shear transport with the clamping action transfer.

Mechanical principle of the stairway. Big beams composed of glass panels connected by the "Zwitserleven" beam detail (see pages 32 – 35).

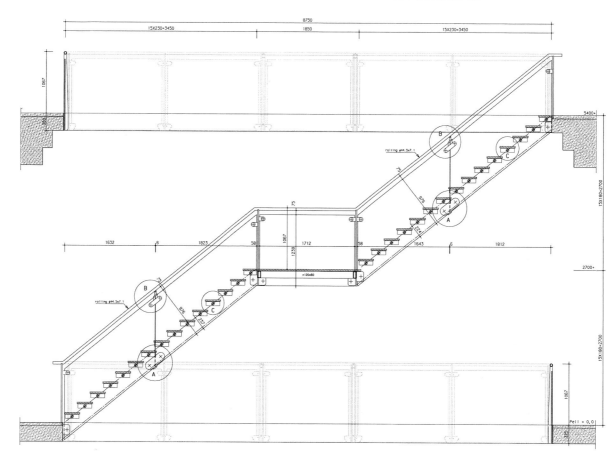

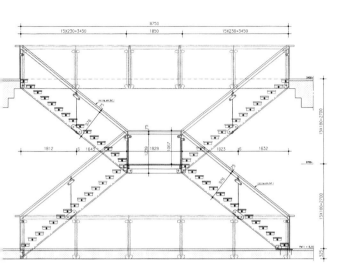

Glass Structure Stairs
– built in Phase 1

"Reinforced" Glass Stairs
– cable system + 4 columns
– built in Phase 2

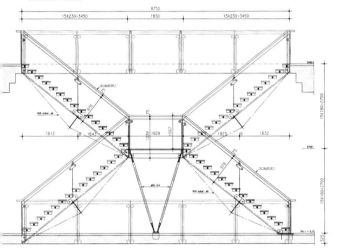

View from under the bridge. The additional steel
columns have little impact on the volume of glass
hovering in the air.

a transparent block enabling the entering visitors a good view at the medieval

church-tower called the Peperbus (pepperbox), situated directly behind the hall.

However, this new hall needed a staircase, and an all-glass staircase was what

Gerard had in mind. He was thinking of a double staircase sharing a landing

halfway. The resulting large X-shape was ideal for longitudinal stability; it could

take up horizontal forces in its plane. By incorporating diagonally crossing

pairs of steel cable bracings directly under the plane of the stair we achieved

transversal stability.

The staircase consisted of two large continuous beams forming

the banisters of the stairs and two centre beams shifting in direction at the plat-

form. The steps were glass panels resting on little brackets glued to the beams.

Since once again the required size exceeded the production limits of laminated

Connection of glass brackets to banisters.
The glass treads are glued to the brackets
and the banisters by silicone; a "soft"
connection to hold the treads in place.

The designers take a rest on the still clear glass (to be sandblasted) of the platform. The steel columns turning this "glass" structure into a "steel" structure are not yet installed, a proof that the original concept worked.

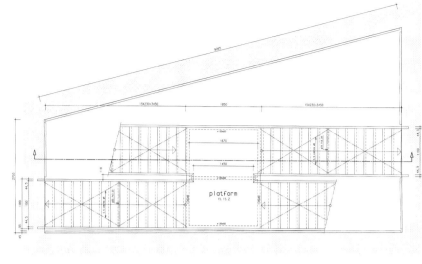

View first floor.

An interesting detail is the support of the steps. Each tread consists of two layers of 15 mm laminated, annealed glass spanning about 1100 mm from one banister to the other. Support is provided by a glass block glued by UV-activated glue to the banisters. As there can be no certainty about the life span of the glue, one bolt connection per step was applied, in the Zwitserleven detailing (see pages 32 – 35), for safety.

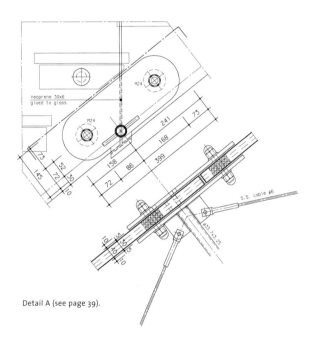

Detail A (see page 39).

glass we had to go back to the "elastic" hole solution suggested for the Zwitserleven big beams. Since this was a complicated structure, a spatial finite element computer program had to calculate all stresses and deformations. The scheme developed for the computer calculation showed that the load on the crossing stairs could be taken up in a very favourable way, resulting in a mainly compressed glass structure. After some time the Alverre firm completed the stairs, and it was a spectacular sight indeed. Everybody shared the joy of having contributed to this innovative structure, which would put Zwolle and its museum on the map of the world.

Then one morning shortly after the completion, people of the museum noticed a big crack in one panel. What or who caused it is still unknown, but the safety concept worked well: despite the big crack the stairs were still

Detail of glued glass bracket. Authorities required a steel bolt to be added.

Connection details of the elements of the glass banister beams.

there and could be walked on without any strange movements, vibrations or whatever. But hell broke loose. The museum wanted to know how safe the structure was compared to steel stairs and described fatal scenarios of school classes falling down into piles of glass fragments. The main contractor claimed he had nothing to do with these stairs since they had been worked out by the architect and another sub-contractor and so on. The most revealing reaction was, however, given by the insurance company, which stated that since they had never heard of a glass staircase they could not have insured it officially. Each meeting added another lawyer to the table, and at last there were far more lawyers present than other professions, let alone engineers. A rabbit had to be conjured out of the hat!

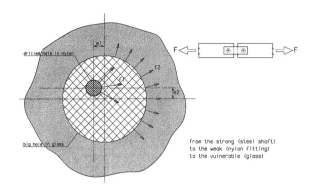

The problem of tolerances was solved by drilling holes in the nylon prop on site.

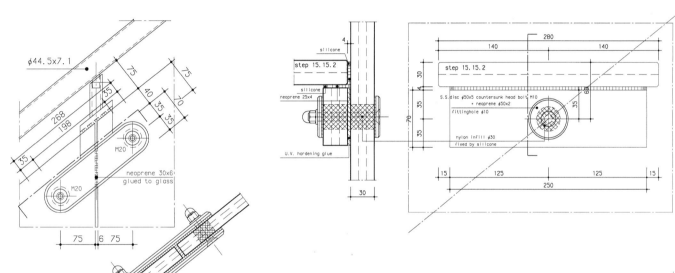

Detail (B) of the complete connection of the glass banister beams.

Detail (C) of the glass brackets supporting the glass treads.

We suggested supporting the landing with four steel columns, and in doing so we emphasized that the load of the staircase would be carried by the steel structure. Everyone agreed to this concept, and despite some reservations of our own, we calculated very accurately the smallest possible steel columns.

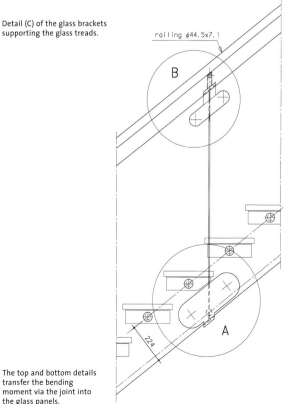

The top and bottom details transfer the bending moment via the joint into the glass panels.

Canopies

Nijmegen, The Netherlands, 1997 – 1999

"A Malicious Hole"

The hole in the glass beam is not polished, so all damages due to drilling affect the stress distribution around the hole. This malicious hole reduced the bearing capacity of the beam enormously.

The modernisation of Nijmegen Station Square brought along several new structures as, for example, an underground parking space for bicycles and a new bus station. Two canopies were to be developed, too, for a taxi stand and for a so-called kiss-and-ride place (where men going to work by train are dropped off by their wives). Since there are already many glass structures on the station square the canopies were to be made of glass as well.

In cooperation with the architects we worked out a single frame of big steel profiles supporting a glass roof cantilevering on both sides. A piece

The primary structure consists of a long, transversal steel beam HEA 300 supported by two steel columns at the perimeter. Glass beams were placed perpendicular to the axis of the HEA beam, cantilevering 2 m and also at a 2 m distance from centre-to-centre. The glass beams have a depth of 400 mm and are composed of 3 x 10 mm laminated float glass panels. On top of the beams horizontal, yet slightly sloped slabs of 2 x 10 mm laminated float glass are mounted and connected to the beams by little stainless steel shoes. The slabs have a rather ambitious span of 2 m centre-to-centre.

Basic cross section Canopy Nijmegen.

1. Steel column HE 300B (clamped in at the foundation).
2. Steel beam (horizontal).
3. Glass beam (continuous).
4. Glass roof panels.
5. Vertical glass panel in gutter (to guide the flow of water).

of cake with our experience, one would think. We calculated the structure, made the drawings and the contractor started to assemble the canopy. However, while erecting the canopy one of the panels of the glass beam broke in one go and the complete beam collapsed after a period of half an hour. A check on our calculations confirmed that with just dead load the stresses should be minimal at 4 N/mm², while average breaking takes place (for short time loading) at about 40 – 60 N/mm². The pattern of the cracks was also very strange: horizontal cracks going vertical after some point and reaching up to the top of the beam. We concluded that a little hole, drilled into the glass beam in order to attach the supports of the roof, had caused the incident. Not only did the hole itself result in a stress-increasing factor of about 3, but examination also showed that the edges of the hole and its inside were very rough and not polished. The very scratchy surface in a place where the tensile stresses were already increased due to the hole itself led to an increase of factor 3 (hole) * 3 (big scratch) * 3 (little scratch in big scratch) = factor 27. The basic stress of 4 N/mm² multiplied by 27 is 108 N/mm², which is too much for the glass. The strange pattern of the cracks, as we later discovered, had been caused by the successive failure of beam-panel 1, beam-panel 2 etc while at the same moment the cantilevering beam started to swing down. (Moment of inertia complete beam I : decreases due to failure of one panel to 2/3 * I : decreases due to two panels broken to 1/3 * I).

So a little hole we had failed to notice had very serious consequences. The client, already somewhat nervous about all these glass issues, understandably insisted on a steel beam instead of a glass one. The glass roof was built as planned, but two small steel cables were added to catch the glass panel

The glass canopy under construction.

The glass beams are supported only at one point in the middle. The attachment of the stainless steel shoe by a hole in the top of the glass beam at the support point proved to be the cause for a premature collapse.

in case it fell down. In retrospect, despite feeling some regret the project taught us never to act too quickly by assuming that a standard glass beam will do the job automatically. Glass itself is not the critical factor. It is always the holes and the edges one has to put an eager eye on!

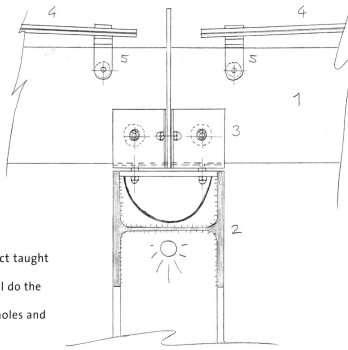

Detail connection glass beam.

1. Glass beam.
2. Steel beam HE 300B (also gutter).
3. Connection steel beam to glass beam.
4. Glass roof panels.
5. Stainless steel connection glass roof to glass beam (the malicious hole).

Glass Bridge for Floriade 2002

Hoofddorp, The Netherlands, 1999 – 2002

"Glass Icicles"

Every four years a large horticultural show in the Netherlands displays show gardens and small parks with much feeling for art. With its small pavilions and follies this exhibition is a real crowd puller. Each Floriade is organised by a different city, which in the end will have a beautiful park which may form, for example, the centre of an exclusive residential area or simply remain a beautiful public park. The rural district of Haarlemmermeer organized the 2002 Floriade and decided to transform the newly designed area into an exclusive business park after the show, a decision partly inspired by the proximity of Schiphol Airport.

Computer generated image at dusk. The shimmering light makes the bridge disappear against the horizon.

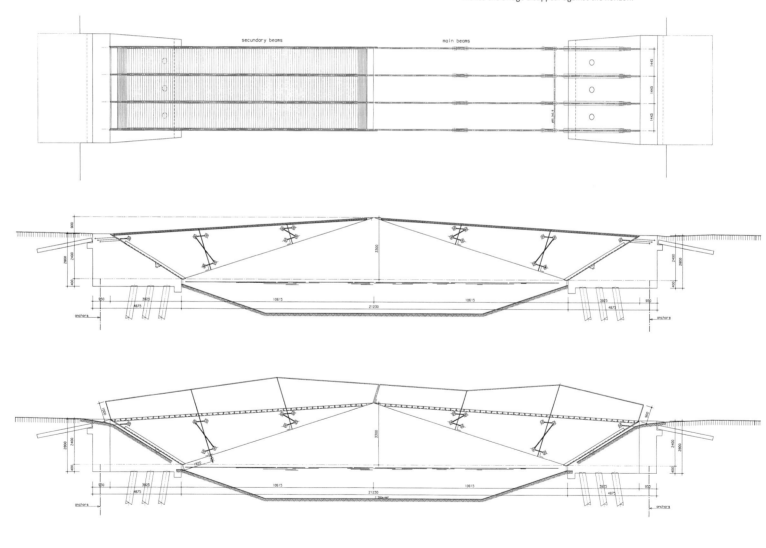

Technical drawing of the composition: two times 5 big beams and some 3,000 secondary, small glass beams.

An unexpected natural model for the glass bridge: an "icicle bridge" by Andy Goldsworthy.

Details of the big glass beam.
The "stitched" connection over the joint
transports both bending moment and
shear force. The small, secondary beams
present an image of a grid floor.

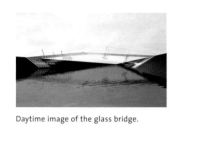

Daytime image of the glass bridge.

The bridge consists of two separate structures, each cantilevering about 10.5 m, so that the total span is about 21 m. Each structure is built up from 6 big glass beams positioned 1 m centre-to-centre. These beams are tapered to emphasize their "just-not-meeting" in the centre of the span. Each beam is composed of 3 panels of glass. Each panel consists of 4 layers of toughened 15 mm glass laminated by resin. The panels werde connected by the same detail as for the Zwitserleven beams (see pages 32 – 35); for the joints the glued-in nylon wads were used again.

A design competition open to graduating architects was held to create a very special bridge crossing the wide waters running along the Floriade area. One of the students, Joris Lüchinger, proposed a project for a full-glass bridge consisting of two halves which were just short of touching in the middle. This bridge not being a bridge was the starting-point for Joris Lüchinger. Another source of inspiration was a photograph of a work by Andy Goldsworthy, an artist who creates objects with materials found in nature. Goldsworthy had made a small "bridge" between two rocks, from two icicles broken off another of his objects and "glued" to the rocks on a wintry day.

The architect contacted ABT/Rob Nijsse for the detailing of this sophisticated structure. Two separate cantilevering structures extend from both sides of the canal to the centre, only just not touching: a gap of a few centimeters remains. Since the width of the water is about 20 m, each piece had to be about 10 m long, which meant that several glass panels had to be connected structurally. The architect decided that the big glass beams used as primary girders should be tapered in order to emphasize their "just-not-meeting" in the centre; their height varies from 2.50 m to 0.15 m. Here we have a structure in which the sign of the stresses is always the same; either tension or compression. And we had to take into account not only a bending moment, with pressure below and tension above in the joints between the panels, but we were also confronted with a shear force to be transported over the joint between the glass plates. So we had to add a diagonal tie.

The floor of the bridge is composed of glass ribs spanning between the main girders. This very special construction, a kind of grid floor so to speak,

The view over the glass bridge a pedestrian, intending to cross it, would have.

The secondary span between the beams is bridged by small beams, height 150 mm, consisting of 2 x 10 mm annealed, laminated glass. These secondary beams are placed with a gap of 30 mm centre-to-centre. They create the floor of the bridge and are connected to the main girders by a stainless steel shoe attached to an inverted U-profile, which neatly slides over the top of the main girder.

Lateral stability is provided by the tensioning of steel cables in the plain of the small beams. In this way the total of 3,000 beams and the steel cables form one stiff horizontal panel connected firmly to the concrete abutments on the banks of the canal.

To avoid buckling out of plane in the compression areas of the big glass beams a stainless steel connecting bar and a steel bracing is attached at the last joint between the glass panels and the concrete abutments.

was tested in practice for safety. It keeps people from slipping when walking or biking. It needs about 3,000 of these little ribs, and their edges must be carefully polished.

The handrails on both sides of the bridge are formed by making the main girder panels project, protecting the top with an inverted stainless steel U-profile.

At the time of writing the use of the glass bridge for the Floriade exhibition is no longer required. It is now meant to be the main entrance bridge to an exclusive business park near Hoofddorp. In mid 2002 the project was stopped due to financial problems as a result of political changes.

Side view of the glass bridge from the bank. The mirrored image in the water is accentuated by the fact that both glass and water are transparent. The technical impression of the connecting details (the stitchings) dominates to the overall impression of what a glass bridge would have looked like. It is a pity that this bridge has not been realized, but let us hope that images like this trigger some other client ...

GLASS FLOORS

"Fortune is like glass – the brighter the glitter,
the more easily broken."

Publilius Syrus, Maxim, 1st century B.C.

Glass stair in the
Arnhem City Hall.

Indoor Floor for a Clubhouse
Arnhem, The Netherlands, 1994 – 1995

Indoor Floor for the Educatorium
Utrecht, The Netherlands, 1994 – 1997

Outdoor Glass Deck
Nijmegen, The Netherlands, 1997 – 1998

Labyrinth "Hildegard von Bingen"
Ruurlo, The Netherlands, 1995 –

Glass Stairs
Arnhem, The Netherlands, 2000 – 2001

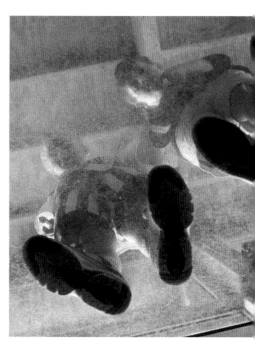

Standing on the walkable hole, two
boys introduce the third dimension
into an ordinary clubhouse.

Glass panels in the floor of a room have been known for quite some time but only in small sizes. However, it was the introduction of a disco dancing floor with coloured lights from underneath in the 1970s movie "Saturday Night Fever" which gave the glass floor a real impulse. Architects began thinking about integrating glass floors into buildings. This implied, of course, that they had to be transparent. Walking on a big transparent floor is thrilling but also very scary to many. Besides cases of open fear of heights (acrophobia), people are afraid because our logic thinking cannot accept the fact that something transparent will carry our weight safely. There is a film made in the 1950s by a big glass firm in which a mother places her baby on a table with half the table top made of glass. She walks around the table and calls her baby to crawl to her over the glass part of the table top. Despite the fact that his mother, a person he loves (we assume), calls him, the baby refuses to crawl across this surface. This behaviour is typical for people who have to walk over a glass floor. Even if the engineer proves that the safety is ten times higher than for a wooden floor, people simply don't trust it. And, admittedly, even I have to take a deep breath before stepping on a transparent floor. Therefore, it is wise to make at least part of a glass floor not transparent but translucent. People feel safer although the difference between a translucent and a transparent glass panel consists in no more than a translucent foil that is only 0.46 mm thick!

Architects and many users are thrilled by the possibility of walking through the air and experience a building in three dimensions. Since safety is a major design criteria it will be clear that all glass floors have to be made from laminated glass. Also we have to be aware of the fact that walking on the glass will create scratches on the surface due to sand or gravel stuck to the soles of shoes. So we have to take care that this scratched zone where you walk does not correspond with a tensile loaded area, for then the scratches would act like stress concentration points resulting in larger stresses in the glass. Often people think of glass as being slippery to walk on. In fact, in dry conditions, it is not slippery at all. Tests have shown that the surface conditions of glass are more or less comparable to natural stone or tiles. When wet, however, glass changes into a potentially slippery surface. One of the ways to avoid this danger is to use a special type of glass that has been given the following treatment.

A glass panel is heated to the point where the surface will become a bit syrupy, melted. Then grains of sand or small parts of broken glass are strewn on it. Due to the more or less molten glass surface they sink halfway in it. After cooling down and rehardening, we have a super-rough surface even when wet. The side effect of this manipulation is that the surface does not wear easily; the strewn-in sand or grains are very well connected to the glass and protect the original glass surface.

This process of melting and rehardening reminds me of an old but unfortunately apocryphal story told in Arab chronicles about the structure of one of the Seven Wonders of the Antique world, the Pharos of Alexandria. This very high and big lighthouse was said to be connected to the rocks of the foundation by "claws of glass". On second thoughts this is not so impossible. Glass can be melted easily and poured into cracks in the rocks. Once solidified, it can take up enormous pressure so it is worthwhile considering a new application of this old construction method.

It would be intriguing to test the connection of glass plates by glass rivets. Steel rivets were used in old steel structures to connect the various steel parts: by putting a heated piece of steel into a hole, hammering it into shape and letting it cool down a steel rivet was made. In this process favourable side-effects were achieved. One was that the more or less molten material filled the holes completely so that no shifting in the connection could occur. The second was that the cooling down of the rivet produced, due to shrinking of the material, a pre-tensioning in the connection enabling a better transfer of forces in it. Because of the high labour costs of this type of connection, the rivets were replaced by cheaper bolts. The same procedure could be applied to glass, resulting in glass "bolts" for glass structures.

Pharos Alexandria
Filling up the cracks in the rocks
with glass.

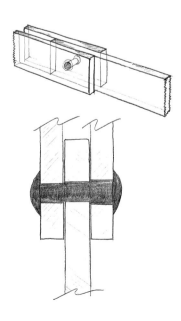

A piece of heated, almost molten,
glass is hammered into the hole to
form a glass rivet.

Indoor Floor for a Clubhouse

Arnhem, The Netherlands, 1994 – 1995

"Walkable Hole"

Sometimes you have the opportunity to be your own client. An interesting position. As it happens I was a member of the building committee for a clubhouse for the Upward Hockey Club in Arnhem. The clubhouse was to have an entrance and dressing rooms downstairs and on top of this a large canteen with a deep terrace overlooking the hockey fields. The budget was tight, so all expenses had to be double-checked. At the same time, a re-evaluation of the notion of safety made all post offices in the Netherlands change from completely closed-off premises into open counters. This meant

The coloured glass façade of the Upward clubhouse, all colours are made by enameling.

This is simply a hole in the first floor, measuring 1 x 1 m. At the edges of the opening a steel angle is mounted in which the glass panel rests. The glass package is 6 mm on top with 2 x 10 mm laminated glass under it. Lamination is by pvb-foils, and the glass is annealed. In order to counteract all uncertainties regarding the use of glass floors in a semi-public space we installed two identical panels on top of each other, each capable of performing the task alone.

Cross section of the glass hole in the floor of the Upward clubhouse.

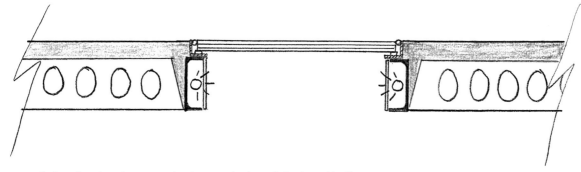

that bullet-proof glass barriers became obsolete and a lot of thick and bullet-proof resistant glass would be available. Of these panels a large glass panel was set into the floor of the canteen above the front door area. This would create a visual upstairs-downstairs link, and at night lateral lights would create a beautiful light pit.

At the beginning naughty boys and dirty old men liked standing beneath to catch glimpses of girls or women passing over their heads, but the wear and tear of the sand on the sports shoes soon changed the panels' quality from transparent to translucent.

After about six years of intensive use the panel shows scratches but no damage whatsoever. It is time to insert a new, transparent one, which of course I had put aside – just to be on the safe side.

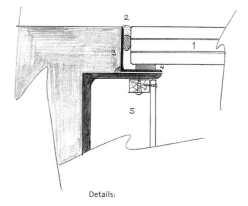

Details:

1. Glass panel (load-carrying).
2. Silicone joint.
3. Steel angle.
4. Neoprene pad.
5. Light in channel.

Indoor Floor for the Educatorium

Utrecht, The Netherlands, 1994 – 1997

"Walkable Void"

The Educatorium is the central facilities building of Utrecht University's Uithof campus. Among several glass structures in the building, there is an all-glass floor at a focal point in the Plexus Solaris of the Educatorium, where two major circulation routes cross on two planes: people walking down the ramp to the restaurant pass under the people who go up another ramp to the lecture rooms or the examination halls. As three-dimensional movement is a vital design feature of the Educatorium, there was a strong architectural desire to visualize it at this central point. Inspiration to use a glass floor came from an

Students walking to the lecture rooms. The effect of the translucent section is visible in the light of the (reflected!) lamplight.

Between two concrete beams glass beams span about 3.50 m, at a distance of 1.50 m from centre-to-centre. The beams are laminated 3 x 10 mm annealed glass. On top of the beams rest the glass floor panels made of 2 x 15 mm annealed glass. A part of the transparent floor panels is made translucent by applying a 0.38 mm thick foil glued on the lower side of the glass. The connection between the glass beams and the horizontal glass panels is only by silicone joint attachment because possible uplift forces will be very small in comparison to the weight of the panels: 75 kg/m².

image of the glass bridge in Rotterdam where the picture was taken from below showing people in the bridge as if flowing in the air (see pages 28 – 29).

The glass floor consists of glass beams, spanning between two concrete beams as primary structure, and horizontal glass panels. The central area of the glass floor is transparent, while the adjacent parts "trodden" by the normal flow of traffic are translucent, providing an alternative passage that respects possible fear of heights and a need for privacy against being seen from below.

On the official inauguration I passed over this glass void with two elderly ladies, who preferred walking on the translucent area and expressed their reluctance of walking on "that thin glass" of the transparent area. Actually they were walking on a glass panel that was hardly thicker at all – only by the very thin foil used to make the transparent glass translucent! Compared to a commonly accepted wooden floor panel of 24 mm plywood the glass floor as used here has a safety factor which is 10 times higher. Human perception is not without prejudice. Wood is familiar, so it is considered safe. Glass is unknown, hence dangerous. A further nice detail is the fact that the connection of the glass panel acts as a balustrade. This is the classical clamping detail. The glass balustrade panel is clamped by bolts and a neoprene interlayer against the structural main beam.

Since this is a public building, authorities were extremely alert to this "dangerous" floor. They requested tests of medieval direness, like dropping a weight of 80 kilos on an area of 10 cm^2 and slinging a sandbag of 70 kilos against the balustrade at a tremendous speed. We checked our calculations and found no reason for doubt but witnessed with some awe the execution of these

tests, which were repeated over and over again. But the structure survived, and after five years of intensive use the panels show some minor surface scratches (on top, hence in the compression area) but no other damage.

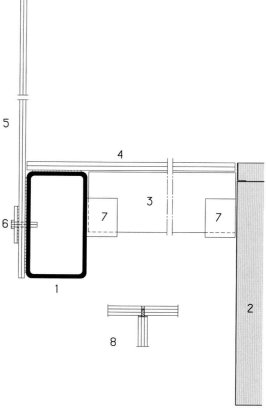

Technical cross section of the Educatorium glass floor.

1. Edge beam, steel hollow section.
2. Concrete floor forming the other edge of the glass floor area.
3. Glass beam.
4. Glass floor panels.
5. Glass balustrade clamped against the steel edge beam.
6. Steel-bolted connection clamping the glass against the steel edge beam.
7. Steel shoe holding the glass beam.
8. Horizontal silicone joint on top of glass beam.

Below and above the glass floor.

Plan of (part of) the first floor of Educatorium:

1. Slope to first floor, inside the building.
2. Slope to first floor, outside the building.
The elements sitting on the slope are art objects
by Joep Lieshout, which light up at night.
3. The glass floor, being the edge of the first floor level.
4. Floor area outside the auditoriums.
5. Auditorium 400 seats.
6. Auditorium 500 seats.

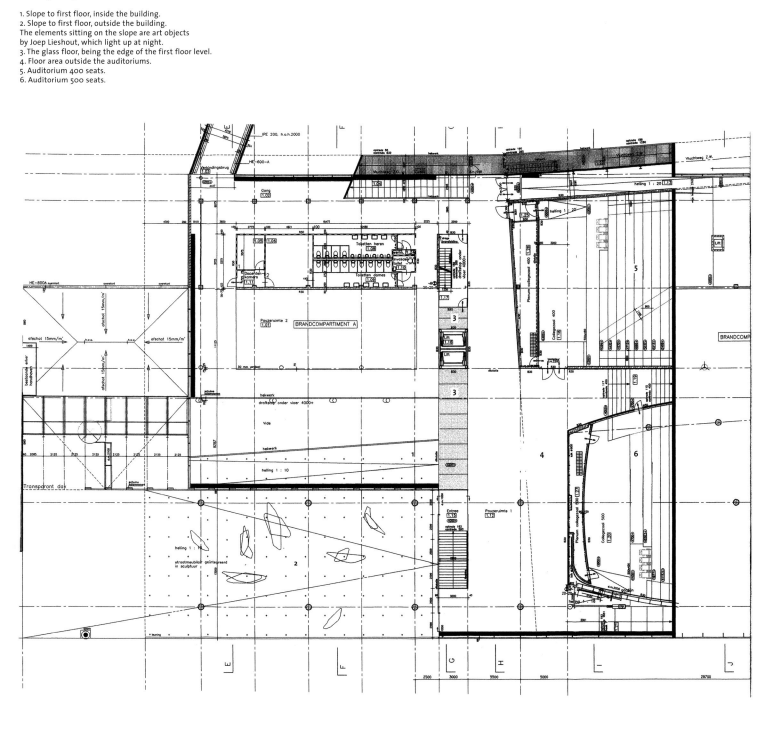

Outdoor Glass Deck

Nijmegen, The Netherlands, 1997 – 1998

"Slippery Ground"

To update the area around the Nijmegen railway station the Dutch architects Cepezed were asked for bright, modern ideas. Part of their plan was an underground bicycle parking facility directly in front of the entrance to the station building. There is a large university in Nijmegen, and before the renovation a large number of bikes had been firmly attached to trees, lampposts, traffic signs or other vertical objects close to the station. The resulting chaotic cityscape undeniably had a romantic touch, but was no longer acceptable to those who dream of the generic clean city.

The critical aspect of using glass outdoors is the danger of slipping in wet conditions. This has been tackled by using a special type of glass called "safety walk" by the glass industry. For the rest it sufficed to make a correct calculation with span, load, allowable stress and deformation, in this case a 1.25 m span and a live load due to a crowd of people of 5 kN/m².
The aspect of the dynamic action of a crowd led to the choice of 2 x 10 mm toughened glass, resting on an elastic neoprene pad and supported by a steel angle. The waterproofing of this detail was very critical. After many similar projects that brought a lot of problems we finally developed the right detail.

Deck of the bicycle parking basement forming the surface of the station square.

The top of this basement facility was to be fitted with glass panels, letting in the daylight, thus providing natural safety in daytime and shining mysteriously up at night. At the same time, the site was located in the main access area to the station, so that all the people bound for the station would have to cross the surface.

Plain glass would have been too slippery, instead we selected a type of glass with a particulary rough surface. To achieve this the glass panel is heated up to the level where the glass starts melting. Sand grains or very small pieces of broken glass are then strewn onto the surface. They sink half-way in and after cooling down create a very rough and strong surface. Of course, since people walk over the glass, the glass was not transparent but translucent.

Laboratory tests proved that only bare feet walking on this glass would cause slipping. The wear and tear of the glass was also tested, and the glass turned out to behave in the same manner as ceramic tiles or some types of natural stone. However, as this was a very intensively used public space, many objections remained. Therefore, a test panel was installed next to the building pit for the basement. This was not a very sensible location for a test because the building pit created a sort of narrow corridor through which all people going to the station had to pass, and together with the sand blowing over from the building pit, this excessive use caused the wear to become visible after some time. Fortunately, the people in charge listened to our arguments, and eventually the glass panels in the roof of the basement were installed. Further experience confirmed that when working with glass it is not the

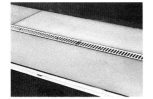

Two glass panels meet in a central gutter providing direct water draining during heavy rainfall.

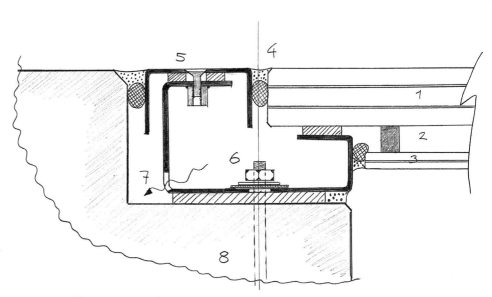

An efficient solution for guaranteed water tightness of the support detail of an exterior glass floor.

1. Glass panel (load-carrying).
2. Cavity.
3. Glass panel (insulating).
4. Silicone joint (first line of defence).
5. Top stainless steel inverted channel profile.
6. Connecting stainless steel profile.
7. Drain to gutter (external).
8. Connection to concrete floor.

material itself, but where and how it is used that creates problems. Here work had obviously not been executed properly, for the first shower of rain resulted in about 100 leaks. Something had gone terribly wrong when the silicone joints were put in. A lot of repairs had to be made.

The overall effect, however, is impressive. The outdoor use of non-slippery glass is one of the many structural possibilities for glass.

Labyrinth "Hildegard von Bingen"

Ruurlo, The Netherlands, 1995 –

"Stairway to Heaven"

In 1998 Hildegard von Bingen would have been 900 years old. She was an extraordinary woman; her music was heavily influenced by intensive religious experiences and is still appreciated today. Quite famous are her visions or ecstasies, passed down through the ages, in which she gave a fascinating description of her religious experiences. One of these visions, a very descriptive and vivid one, is about a layered labyrinth from which you have to find your way out by praying. Labyrinths are a major motif in the heathen and Christian spiritual tradition, not only as a literary image, but even in built form.

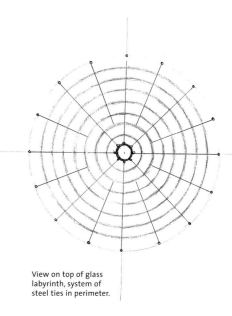

View on top of glass labyrinth, system of steel ties in perimeter.

The main structure is a central core that houses the elevator and the stairway. Compression rings made of steel tubes are suspended from this core by means of steel bars. The tubes carry rounded glass walls of 2 x 15 mm toughened glass, which also form the balustrades. At the same time, the tubes support the glass floors, which are also attached to the glass walls. The floors are circular-shaped (laser-cut) annealed glass panels of 2 x 10 mm.

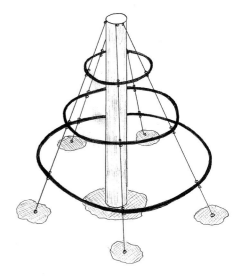

Detail of integration steel structure and glass structure.

Here is an excerpt from Hildegard's vision, translated from her original Latin:

"Afterwards a gigantic image appeared / round and shimmering. / At the top it ended in one point / shaped like an egg. / In the centre it became wider / and at the bottom it reclined again. / The outer layer which surrounded it / was made of radiant fire. / Under this a dark layer. / In the radiant fire a reddish, / sparkling sphere of fire floated about, / so big that it illuminated the entire structure. / Three lights burned over it. / They gave the image volume and balance / with their glow, so it did not become obscure. / Now and then the fiery sphere came to / the foreground and many fires sprayed / their flames in its direction, / so it glowed up even more. / Sometimes the sphere itself went / down, but it felt so cold down there, / that it quickly pulled back its flames. / From the radiant fire-zone / which surrounded the structure a whirlwind rose. /

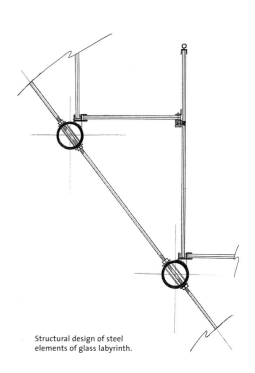

Structural design of steel elements of glass labyrinth.

And also in the dark layer below / a wind was born, / which, with its whirls, engulfed the structure. / In this layer an intense, / obscure fire glowed, / so horrible that I could not look into it. / It raged so furiously that / it made the whole layer shake, for / it was full of noise, stormy winds and / clattering, pointed stones, / big and small."

An old clergyman, father Henri Boelaerts, took up this idea, this vision and wanted to create such a labyrinth as a real building. He made a sketch and a model of it and I was asked to transform it into a real structure, using glass as the main material. This was an awkward experience. To combine a technical solution with a spiritual concept requires more then a sheer design, for one ought to be able not only to understand the concept but also to undergo the experience to some extent.

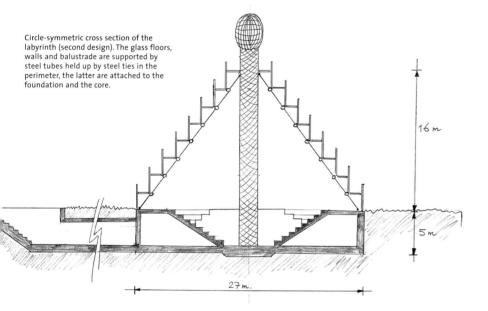

Circle-symmetric cross section of the labyrinth (second design). The glass floors, walls and balustrade are supported by steel tubes held up by steel ties in the perimeter, the latter are attached to the foundation and the core.

Model made by father Henry Boelaerts. The penciled line shows a possible way to reach the top of the structure through prayer and meditation.

Drawing of the vision of Hildegard von Bingen by a monk, as approved by Hildegard von Bingen.

Basically, the structural design calls for a steel structure, pointing to the centre of the earth as a reminder of the starting-point of the visitor whose praying pilgrimage into the labyrinth is about to begin. It is arranged on several levels, and at each level the visitor follows a glass circle before taking one step up to the next level. After six circles the top is reached.

A location for the structure was offered by the Dutch town of Ruurlo, but the financing of the project proved to be too difficult. Therefore, a new approach was worked out, based on hanging compression rings. Realizing this structure would bring an exciting contribution of structural engineering with glass to the world of art and religious culture.

Glass Stairs

Arnhem, The Netherlands, 2000 – 2001

"Firemen's delight"

Minimal use of material. Columns support each end of the tread to minimize deflection.

Glass treads emerging mysteriously from a natural stonewall.

Back view.

The stair is attached to the structural core of the building consisting of a 200-mm-thick brick wall. Brick is not a very strong material. Therefore, a steel hollow section (160 x 160 mm) was mounted to the brick wall. Two "tails" were welded to the hollow section reducing the support forces on the brick wall. On top of this steel beam the clamping detail for the glass treads was attached. Each detail can adjust the height and rotation of the tread.

View when standing on the glass stairs. A sand-blasted stripe prevents the danger of slipping.

The city of Arnhem suffered heavily in the Second World War. The centre, near the famous "one bridge too far", was completely destroyed in the September days of 1944. After the war a new, modernistic city hall was built in this area. After 50 years of service a modernization of the building had to be done. Not only the services and the insulation of the city hall had to be improved, but also fire escape routes had to be reconsidered. For this reason an extra stairway to the ground floor had to be created near the main entrance. This was a delicate location, very visible, near the place where all people were supposed to enter the building.

Architect Ed Morroy of the architectural office AGS suggested an all-glass stair. The stair leads around a structural core housing the elevator and air-ducts. In the architectural design the core was clad with marble, and the

A strong steel detail, hidden in the natural stone wall, holds each glass tread.

Four bolts and neoprene pads allow for all tolerances and necessary corrections in height.

A structure of steel hollow sections connected to the wall (to be clad with natural stone) supports the cantilevering treads to the bearing brick wall.

The intended effect of glass treads coming out of a natural stone wall. An example of good design, good detailing and good craftsmanship during the execution.

glass treads were meant to come mysteriously out of the granite wall. No other structural parts should be visible.

This required clever detailing, as especially the cantilevering of the tread out of the wall is a structural issue for a torsion moment. There was also the requirement that the treads should be adjustable in height and that even the replacement of a broken tread should be possible. Using parts of our detailing worked out for Hengelo (see pages 132–133), we changed this detail into an adjustable one achieved through a narrow opening, a slit, in the granite-clad wall. Attaching a steel hollow section to the brick wall of the core solved the problem of taking up the torsion moment. To get a good grip on the brick wall, two steel "tails" were welded to the hollow section. On top of this hollow section the steel detail to hold the cantilevering glass treads was mounted.

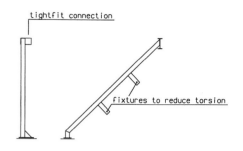

Front view and side view of the hidden steel beam allowing the glass treads to cantilever from the wall.

The glass treads are made of laminated glass, 3 x 15 mm toughened glass, and a top layer of 10 mm annealed glass. This top layer is not a part of the structure.
To minimize the deformation of the cantilevering tread, small glass columns were placed under the end of each tread. Since these columns go down all the way to the ground floor, the treads actually do not cantilever anymore but rest on two supports.

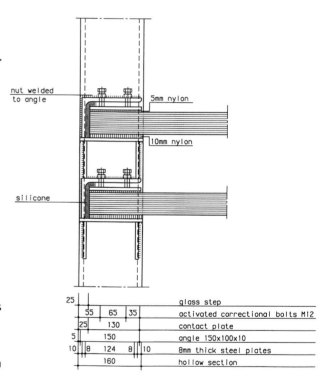

Clamping detail of glass tread in/on the steel beam. Corrections of position are possible, good care has also been given to a flexible, soft transfer of concentrated forces in this crucial detail.

The glass treads consisted of 3 x 15-mm-thick, toughened glass and an annealed top, 10 mm thick, cantilevering 1,300 mm. After the glass treads were mounted the bending of the treads was "noticeable". The deflection at the upper end with a 100 kg person on it was 22 mm, which was considered too much and alarming for users. Also the idea of a glass, hence transparent stair combined with this sensing of motion met heavy resistance. Eventually, we decided to place small glass columns under the end of each step forming a continuous support to the ground. The cantilever was no more, and the bending of the treads was reduced to almost nothing. The visual impact of this addition was minimal.

Front view. The considerable thickness of the treads results from the required bearing capacity of 3 kN/m² of dynamic load (people fleeing in emergencies).

GLASS COLUMNS

"Design never starts with calculation. The form is determined through inspiration. Calculation simply confirms the designer's original intuition."

Eduardo Torroja (1899 – 1961)

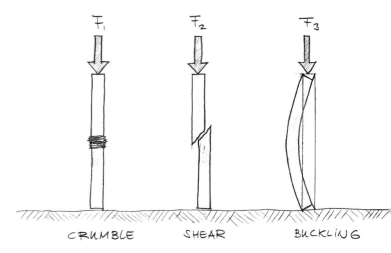

The three ways in which a column may collapse.

Glass Truss Elements for an Office Building
Amstelveen, The Netherlands, 1994 – 1996

Spiral Staircase in the ABT-Office
Arnhem, The Netherlands, 1997 –

Composite Column (Concept)
Utrecht, The Netherlands, 1998

Variations on a Column
Holten, The Netherlands, 1993 and Seoul, Korea, 1997

Case Study: A Realized Glass Column
Saint-Germain-en Laye, France, c. 1994

Tularosa Glass Tower Project
A Basin in the Western Part of the USA, 1999

A Glass Column Solution, ABT-Office
Arnhem, The Netherlands, 2000

Glass Beam for Conservatory
Leiden, The Netherlands, 2001 – 2002

Supercolumn (Concept)
1996, not realized

Crumbling.

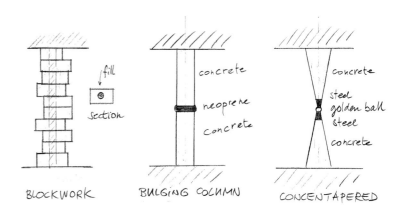

While we have been able to make glass floors, glass roofs, glass walls and glass beams, the last structural element still resisting its transformation into glass is the column.

In general, a column is a difficult element in a structure. Architects and clients do not like columns; they stand in the way and they block the view. If it is impossible to reduce them in number, architects ask them to be made as small as possible. Structural engineers, by contrast, love columns: they reduce the span of beams and floors, and make structures less complicated. How to overcome this aversion by the architects? I like to quote from a text by Le Corbusier on his Villa Savoye: "Proudly they stand a-straight the columns; the soldiers of architecture, carrying their load." This mostly helps a little since no one dares to contradict so great an architect as Le Corbusier.

But engineers should make columns more attractive, too. One way to do this is to make their shape more expressive, which I tried for instance in a study on the shape of columns for the restaurant of the Educatorium project (see pages 84 – 85). As a starting-point for the structural design of these columns we agreed with the architect to take up the question: how do columns collapse?

There are three ways in which columns can collapse. The first one is by crumbling, slowly yielding under too big a compression load. The second is by buckling, by suddenly breaking in the middle. This case is most of the times the critical one. The third is by breaking due to shear force; sliding along each other. I made a number of column designs related to each collapse shape. The intention was to choose a typical column for each location and thereby give the space around the column identification. Unfortunately, the cold wind of financial constraints only led to a variation in size and in a round or square cross section with an identical cross-shaped column (the so-called Mies van der Rohe quotation).

Another way to make columns more attractive and less repulsive to architects would be to make them out of glass. Although glass performs well under compression, there is the danger of buckling, which makes it hard to conceive a safe glass column. Buckling will result in tensile stresses and the miniature cracks will play their spoilsport role. Therefore, safe structural glass elements have to be double, triple or more. If one part fails for whatever reason, the remaining parts must still be able to carry the load so that the damaged element can be replaced. But will a glass column not be the utmost achievement in applying glass structurally? Imagine high-rise buildings resting on mysteriously shining beams of light (bear in mind the immense potential bearing force of glass); a dream would have come true. Theoretical aspects of how to make a glass column are set out in this chapter, and the examples shown allow glimpses at how a future glass column may look. The journey on the road to realize this has, however, only just begun.

Laboratory test on massive glass bar.   Laboratory test on glass cylinder.

Buckling.

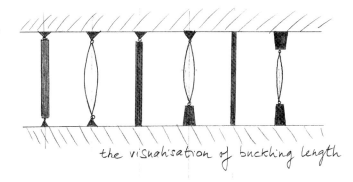

the visualisation of buckling length

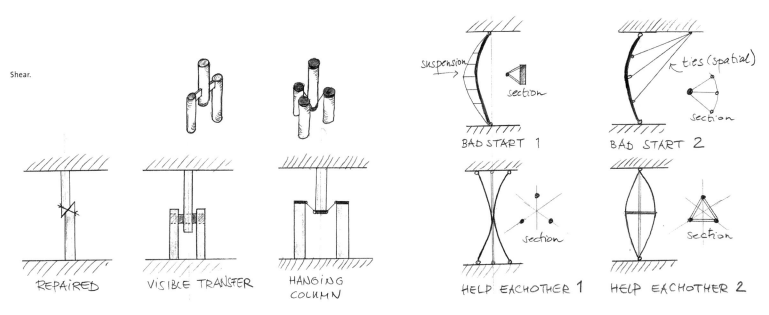

Shear.

REPAIRED   VISIBLE TRANSFER   HANGING COLUMN

suspension   section   ties (spatial)   section
BAD START 1   BAD START 2

section   section
HELP EACHOTHER 1   HELP EACHOTHER 2

Glass Truss Elements for an Office Building

Amstelveen, The Netherlands, 1994 – 1996

"Maximum-Transparency Roof"

While the projected glass beams for the Zwitserleven building were unfortunately not realised (see pages 32 – 35), there was a successful glass structure inside the same building: the roof structure of the restaurant. Here it is possible to catch a glimpse of the glass column concept.

As the span of the restaurant roof was only about 5 m, several alternative solutions were developed, at the architect's instigation, to enhance its visual attractiveness. In the end a glass truss was opted for. The principle of the glass truss is mechanically dictated: in a one-field span the nature of the

The W-shaped truss is composed of steel and glass elements. The top member is a steel hollow section with a width of 80 mm (120 x 80 x 5 mm steel profile) supporting and connecting the insulated glass panels forming the roof. The compression-loaded parts of the truss are of massive borosilicate glass bars 30 mm in diameter, the steel cables are 10 mm in diameter. The difficult connection of a glass bar to a steel cable was solved in a beautiful detail.

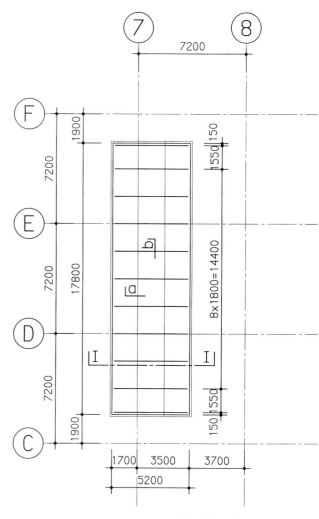

Plan of glass roof.

View from under the glass truss of the Zwitserleven restaurant roof in Amstelveen.

forces in the diagonals is always either tensile or compressive. Normally, all diagonals in a structure are of identical dimension, from which results one anonymous type of bar, no matter whether the diagonal is placed near the support (heavy load) or halfway in the centre of the span (small load). In order to show the nature of the internal forces, we suggested here to use minimized high-quality steel bars for the tensile forces and the optimal option for the compressive forces: glass! Glass is an ideal material for compression elements; the only danger for failure comes from buckling, which means that a correct calculation of the dimensions would lead to a completely safe structure.

Two problems were raised by this decision. What would happen if a glass bar (caused by whatever reason) broke? And what should be the connection of a glass bar to a steel cable? Using a hollow section for the upper edge to

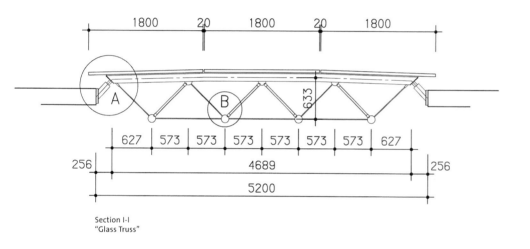

Section I-I
"Glass Truss"

The sequence of glass trusses, combined with the rhythm of glass bars and steel bars in the trusses, weaves a shining restaurant roof structure.

support the insulated glass panels of the horizontal roof (with an inner gutter like the one used in the Budapest building, see pages 24–27) solved the first question. This steel profile was so strong that if a glass bar broke the hollow section would be able to carry (on its own) the roof with a 1.1 safety factor. In such an emergency the roof would bend through significantly but would not come down, so that repairs could be effected. As to the connection between a glass bar and a steel cable, flexibility was an issue, as well as making sure that the diagonals were hinged perfectly so as to avoid clamping moments. The solution was found in gluing a stainless steel cap to both ends of a glass bar and making the connection in a central node, which would be pulled together by tightening the screw-thread of the steel elements. It is vital to avoid direct contact of glass and steel, therefore neoprene rings and pads were inserted into the stainless steel cap. Although the idea came up that an even bigger hollow section could do the job all on its own, the client had the courage to decide in favour of the glass truss. Perhaps it helped that each glass bar, with both caps glued on, was tested in the laboratory (the same procedure as for the column in a villa, see pages 69 – 70).

Later the same strategy of exposing the nature of the diagonal forces was used for the big truss spanning 35 m in the Educatorium in Utrecht. And there is another structure paying tribute to this truss in that same building: the same type of massive bars was applied in the ladder-frames of the C-500 lecture room. There the test results of the Amstelveen glass bars were very helpful in convincing the Utrecht client of the safety of these glass elements (see pages 32 – 35).

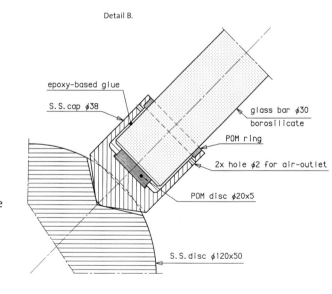

Detail B.

The light caught in the glass bar gives an extra feature to the structure. Especially at night the trusses seem to "light up".

In the Amstelveen building, especially at night, the massive bars catch the light and make the structure look as if made out of light-carrying bars. But more importantly, this glass bar-type element represented for me the first, in a sense hidden, glass column!

Detail C.

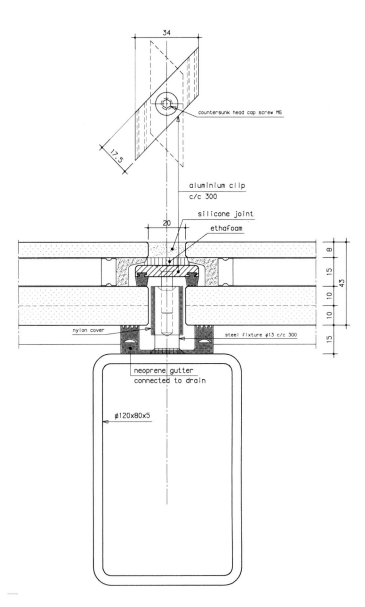

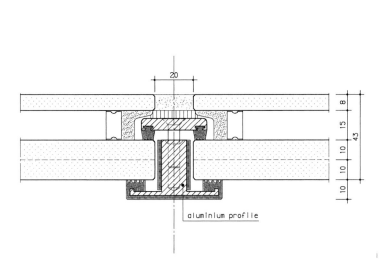

An essential detail for both the Budapest project and the Amstelveen project we developed to connect an insulated glass panel to a glass beam (Budapest) or a steel hollow section (Amstelveen). For this purpose the separation between the two glass panels to produce the void in between them is placed inward to create space for the mechanical connection. An oblique piece of steel is pushed through the gap on top and then rotated in the created space. A screw fixes the steel element and claps the insulated glass panel to the glass beam/ steel hollow section.

The clamping force produces a first barrier against water penetration by compressing the neoprene strips in this connection. A silicone joint between the two top glass panels provides the second barrier against water penetration. The whole technical connection is hidden in the joints between the two insulated glass panels.

Spiral Staircase in the ABT-Office

Arnhem, The Netherlands, 1997 –

"The Stapled Structure Approach"

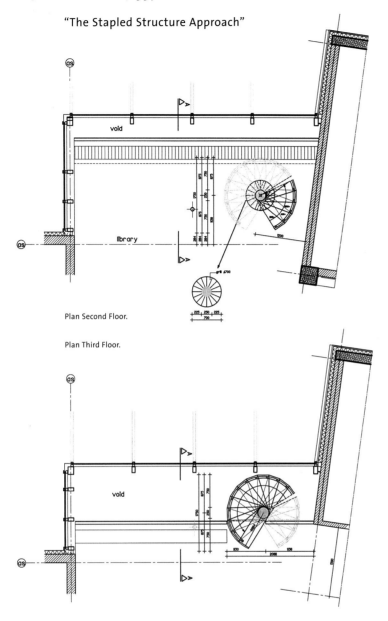

Plan Second Floor.

Plan Third Floor.

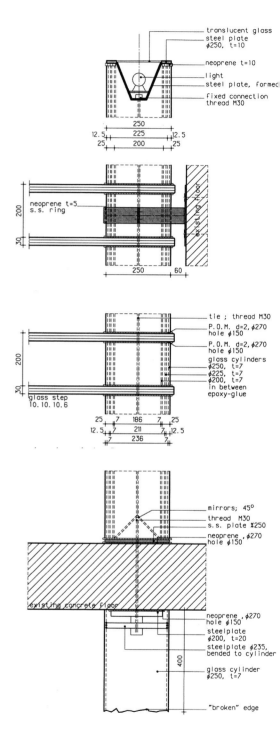

Details 1 – 4.

For connecting two floors of the rapidly growing ABT practice I was given the far from easy assignment to design an all-glass staircase. The available space was very limited, so that it had to be a spiral staircase to be used by only one person at a time. The column principle lead to the conception of the axis of the staircase as a series of stacked glass cylinders. This stacked structure was created by making small column (= cylinder) parts – the height of one tread – establishing a column-tread-column-tread sequence, in which the glass treads spiralled up around the glass column. A system of glass bars as poles and a set of steel cables as balustrade provided a virtually immaterial structure.

Since this staircase was to be close to a façade adjacent to an important motorway we included a strong floodlight under the column to make the staircase shine at night.

As could be expected, the detailed estimate for construction costs was very high. And an alternative estimate for a (boring) steel staircase proved to be five times lower than that for the price of the glass construction. A weighted choice was quickly made.

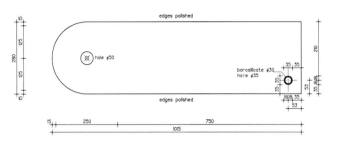

edges polished

hole ⌀50

borosilicate ⌀30
hole ⌀35

edges polished

Glass tread.

The central axis of the staircase was to consist of glass cylinders, one step high, each made from three elements (round 250, 225 and 200 mm respectively, each t = 7 mm) laminated to each other by transparent glue. On top of a cylinder a glass tread (2 x 10 mm annealed laminated glass) was placed, cantilevering 1 m from the central axis, on top of which came the next part of the axis and so on. The top of this stack was connected to the upper floor in order to provide stability, and a tensioned cable in the centre of the cylinder prestressed away all possible tension due to bending of the central axis.

The banister consists of slender massive glass bars, round 30 mm, glued into each step and a spatially curved stainless steel tube, round 40 mm, set on top of the glass bars as a handrail. Strong lights under the floor and reflecting mirrors placed at 45° send a bundle of light up through the central glass axis.

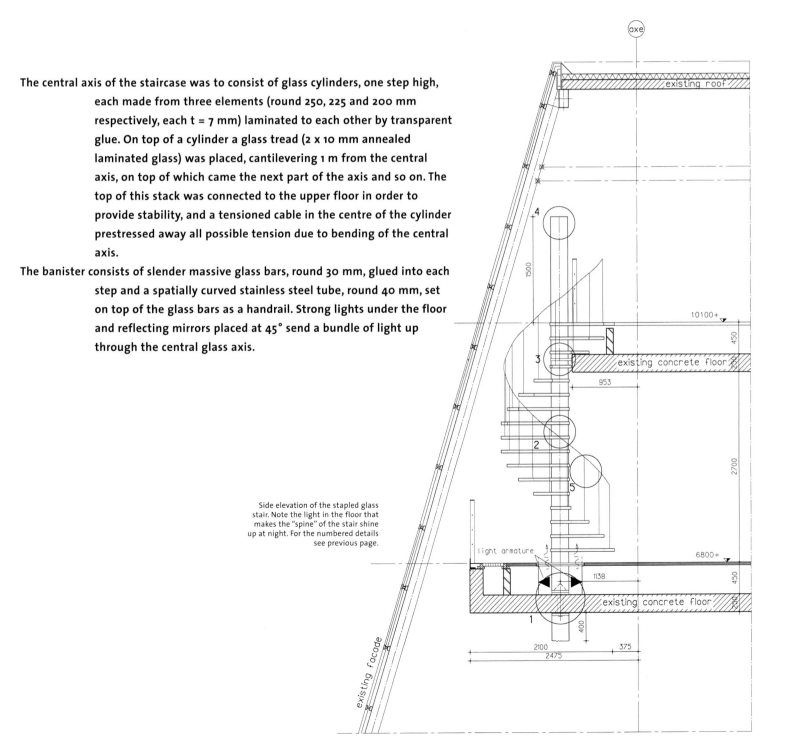

Side elevation of the stapled glass stair. Note the light in the floor that makes the "spine" of the stair shine up at night. For the numbered details see previous page.

Composite Column (Concept)

Utrecht, The Netherlands, 1998

"Concrete Glass"

The Utrecht University campus, which also houses the Educatorium and the Minnaert Building, was to have a new library. It was planned as a spatial mix of depots and reading or computer rooms that involves a mixture of concrete and glass in terms of building materials. The intention was to give the building an advanced technical look, and several scenarios in this vein were developed with the architect Wiel Arets in a number of brainstorm sessions. The most important structural issues were the façade (see page 95) and a design of a glass roof (see page 135).

Formwork around the glass-covered column to enable good pouring of the concrete.

1. Outside part of formwork to keep the real formwork panels (2) in place.
2. Real formwork panels.
3. Glass panels (steel threads glued on for anchoring).
4. Silicone joint.
5. Open corner (variation on 4).
6. Structural concrete, reinforced column.

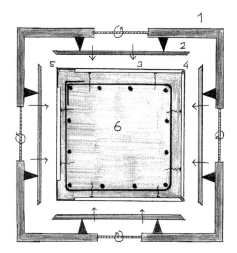

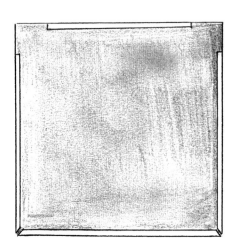

The resulting concrete/glass column.

But there was also another surprising idea, born in one of these sessions: to cast concrete in "a glass formwork". This would not only create a strange reflecting surface for the concrete, it would also produce natural-looking frozen patterns created by the flow of the concrete during pouring. The resulting concrete column itself is the structural part of this proposal, while the glass is only "the skin". Since the glass would have to be very thick to carry the big load of the still liquid concrete during pouring, a solution has been worked out in which traditional formwork is combined with permanent glass panels attached directly to the outside of the concrete. Toughened glass should be used because it is capable of taking up concentrated loads resulting from bumping against or beating the column.

The image that may occur if concrete were to be poured into a glass box. Notice the fine streaming patterns in the concrete and the different shades of colouring in the concrete itself.

Variations on a Column

Holten, The Netherlands, 1993 and Seoul, Korea, 1997

Holten, 1993: "The Bundle Approach"

Information from non-structural technical fields such as shipbuilding, the machine-building industry, biology or the chemical industry can provide fruitful inspiration. An ad of the German firm Schott advertizing glass tubes and bars to be used in the chemical industry made me dream once more of the glass column.

This coincided with an idea that OMA pursued at the same time. They were working on a villa in the Netherlands where they wanted to replace a steel corner-column, which was blocking the view, with a glass one. Of the three

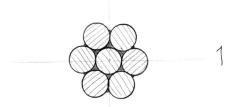

bundle of bars
"Holten" concept

A image of how the "Holten" column would have looked.

proposals I developed – a laminated rectangular column, laminated layers of glass cylinders and a bundle concept of 7 massive bars – Rem Koolhaas on architectural grounds chose the bundle concept. It was agreed with the authorities that there would be laboratory tests exposing the complete glass column to a load three times as high as the highest possible real load according to standards. Later I learnt that when building Crystal Palace the same was done for all the cast-iron beams, which were used for the very first time on a large scale on this occasion.

When the glass column was ready to be installed, the house was almost finished: the immense glass façade had been put in, the false ceiling had already been closed and the client was eager to move in. But this was normal practice at OMA, and the client was convinced that this improvement to his house was necessary. So it was decided to take the steel column out. To this purpose the

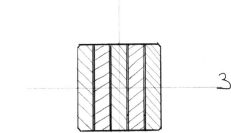

The three ways to create a safe laminated glass column.

1. Bundle of massive glass bars, glued together.
2. Cylinders glued together.
3. Rectangular glass panels, laminated.

roof was hoisted and I instructed Jeroen Thomas of OMA to knock on the steel

column during lifting: a change of pitch would indicate that the column was not

carrying the roof anymore and could be taken away safely. But the pitch did not

change. When the only results achieved were cracking noises in the ceiling and

the façade, the effort was stopped. An inspection of the connection between the

column and the roof beams revealed that the column had been welded to the

roof beams instead of bolted as had been indicated in the technical drawings.

Afraid of serious damage, the client abandoned the attempt. I felt extremely

disappointed, so disappointed that I could not forget the concept. I designed

an all-glass coffee table using the "remains" of this glass column concept for

the table-legs, so the column concept is now forever present in my living room.

The column for a villa in the Netherlands had to carry a load of 35 kN (with safety factor 1.5), its length was 2.9 m. Three strategies were proposed:
– a stack of 7 annealed glass strips, total width 70 mm, each 10 mm thick, with the strips glued together by resin;
– a bundle of 7 massive bars, each 30 mm in diameter, leading to a total diameter of about 90 mm, with the bars glued together by UV-activated glue;
– a lamination of two cylinders, the outer one 100 mm in diameter and 8 mm thick, the inner 75 mm in diameter and 10 mm thick. The gap of 4.50 mm between the two cylinders was to be (partly!) filled by epoxy glue. The right type is still to be found.

A closer look at the bundled column, giving a good impression of how a bundled-glass column would look. The column is not transparent but seems to deform the light into a concentrated bundle as well.

Live load test on the bundled column concept: the Nijsse family coffee table.

Connection detail of the Korea column. It was proposed to let water flow through the column for fire-proofing.

Seoul, 1997: "The Layer Approach"

The glass column had not disappeared from OMA's memory, and a few years later the suggestion came to make glass columns for the Samsung Museum in Seoul, Korea. We worked out a concept for the glass cylinder, this time opting for a structure layered like an onion. The overall structural concept combined both glass and concrete columns. If the glass columns failed, their load could be distributed on the rest of the (concrete) structure. Fire-proofing was achieved by a system of water being pumped around through the columns. In the case of fire, water is pumped through the glass column and keeps the column cool, thus preserving its integrity. The proposal was detailed down to a beautiful detail for the connection to the floor the column was supposed to carry. However, the collapse of the Korean economy prevented these glass columns from being built.

A 1:10 scale model of the "Korea" column, made by OMA. Column caps are shaped in such a way as to make a hinge.

The columns for the Samsung Museum had to carry loads from 120 to 310 kN and varied in length from 2.50 m to up to 4 m. They were designed as laminations of two cylinders, the outer one 300 mm in diameter and 20 mm thick, the inner one 250 mm in diameter and 20 mm thick. The gap between the two cylinders was again to be partly filled with epoxy glue.

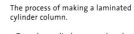

cylinder 1
cylinder 2
glue filled space

"Corea" concept

The process of making a laminated cylinder column.

1. Two glass cylinders: one placed within the other.
2. Filling the small gap between the two cylinders with a two-component glue.
3. After hardening of the glue: a safe, laminated glass column.
4. Perfect central positioning is not necessary!

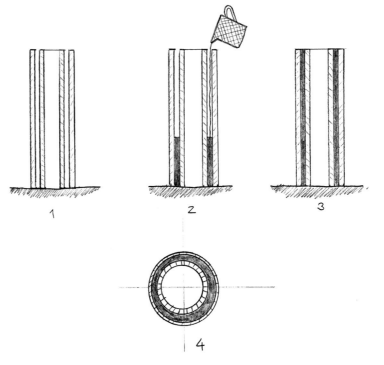

Case Study: A realized Glass Column

Saint-Germain-en-Laye, France, c. 1994

"Glass Cross (to be carried)"

The top detail of the glass column. Steel plates connected to the roof beams hold the top of the glass columns. For security reasons the middle part of the three layers of glass of each panel stops before the outer two, in this way the middle one is much more protected, especially the vulnerable outside edge.

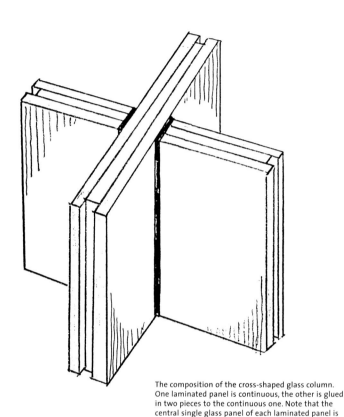

The composition of the cross-shaped glass column. One laminated panel is continuous, the other is glued in two pieces to the continuous one. Note that the central single glass panel of each laminated panel is recessed to be effectively protected.

For a number of years one of the first glass columns in the sense discussed here is 'on show' in the townhall of the small French town of Saint-Germain-en-Laye near Paris.

Accessible through a wide corridor, in the centre of a beautiful light-filled space, there is a central glass patio – part of an inverted cone of bent glass –, which is surrounded by a roof resting on glass columns. According to my expert analysis, in the case of a collapse of one or even all glass columns, a structural steel system in the roof would hold the construction, partly by means of a tension ring around the patio. In the case of a structure as experimental as a glass column this is certainly a wise decision. The slight envy I felt made me think that this principle would not have been applied to steel columns. What makes a glass column a genuine structural column?

The columns themselves are beautiful cross-columns in the best Mies van der Rohe tradition, well-made and blessed with expert details.

So the first glass column in the world is already built. But on the other hand, a glass column as I understand it is something else. It is a mysterious shining beam of light, effortlessly carrying the building above it. The cross-shaped pattern of this structure is problematic, as the magic of the glass, that is its transparency, is lost because of the puzzling reflections of the planes and the blackening of the glass when looked at edgeways-on. A glass cross-column is not mysteriously absent – and is, therefore, not a good glass column as we understand it.

The height of the column is 3.20 m. Each section of the cross consists of three panels, of which the middle one is receding slightly, so that it is fully protected by the other two. The two outer planes of glass are 10 mm and the central panel 15 mm float glass. The maximum loading that can occur is calculated to be 69 kN. A one-to-one test proved the ultimate load – at the moment before, as it can be so poetically described, fatal loss of coherency – to be 430 kN.

The inner court of the city hall.
An inverted glass cone with a
wintergarden surrounded by
a roof carried by glass columns.

The cross-shaped glass column
supporting the steel roof beams.

Tularosa Glass Tower Project

A Basin in the Western Part of the USA, 1999

"Glass Earth"

During a scholarship at Schloss Solitude in Stuttgart, Germany, the Irish artist Patti O'Neill pursued a project based on her fascination with the beauty of the landscape ensuing from a river grinding its way into the earth for millions of years. The Grand Canyon in the United States is the ultimate example of this phenomenon. Her proposal for a work of art was to set a glass tower into such a gorge, the height of the tower equalling the depth of the gorge. It would be a transparent tower, without visible structural elements. Coloured synthetic panels were to be placed inside the tower as if they were echos of the layers of

The 35-m-high tower has a cross section of 7 x 7 m. The walls are made of 3 x 15 mm toughened glass. The size of each glass panel is 3.50 x 4.50 m. The laminated panel edges are shaped in such a way that they slide into each other and hence are capable of taking up horizontal forces. The resistance of the tower against bending due to the wind is secured by pre-tensioned steel cables (round 10 mm) hidden in the corners and in the centre of each wall so that there are no steel cables on the outside. The weight of the glass combined with the pre-tensioning is to counterbalance the tensile forces summoned by the wind.
A corner detail connects the vertical steel cable with a horizontal steel bar (round 4 mm) which pulls the panels actively together and secures the form of the tower.

the earth that appear on the walls of the gorge. After difficulties in acquiring permission for her ideas in Germany, the artist asked us to develop a preliminary, but realistic structural design as a basis for the fund-raising phase of her project. This implied that there were no means available for research, calculation and drawing activities, but although the project was still rather vague, the idea appealed to me, and the challenge to create a tower consisting almost entirely of glass was a great inspiration.

The structural design principal was developed with much support by one of ABT's most creative draughtsmen, John Broere. With his common sense and feel for construction he played a major role, not only in this instance but in many other projects as well. Not only did he put our feet firmly on the ground every now and then, but he also came up with some very clever details.

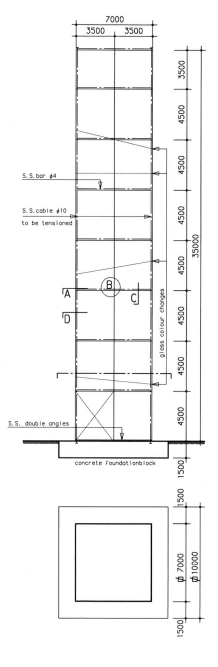

Elevation and section of the Tularosa glass tower. Stacked glass panels compressed by stainless steel bars form the structure of the tower and can take up the horizontal loads from the wind.

The buildable, full-glass tower gradually emerged and was given a virtual site, the Tularosa Basin in New Mexico, USA.

Patti O'Neill curated an attractive presentation/exhibition in Berlin and made a video with artistic, hence difficult, images and sounds. While the project has remained unrealized at the time of writing, we at ABT have learned much we can now use in other projects.

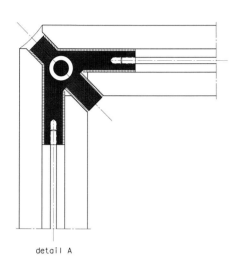

detail A

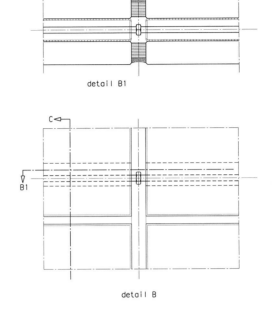

detail B1

C

B1

detail B

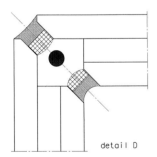

detail D

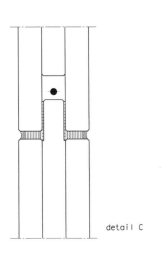

detail C

Model. The glass panels change colours by means of a coloured pvb-foil holding the laminated glass panels together.

A Glass Column Solution, ABT-Office

Arnhem, The Netherlands, 2000

"Glass Reception"

The ABT building in Velp, Netherlands.

Going the way chosen by many architects when starting their careers, I became my own client creating the technological *tour de force* of a glass column at the ABT office. Beautifully situated in the woodland hills of the eastern Netherlands, the modern ABT building is an appreciated presence in an one-and-a-half-century-old scenery. It is located on the site of a former large villa which was part of an ensemble of villas built between 1850 and 1910 for clients who had made their fortune in the Dutch colony of the East Indies, the present Republic of Indonesia. The shape of the ABT building is inspired by the volume of the earlier villa.

The glass column of the bundled type consists of 7 massive bars round 30 mm, the central one surrounded by the other 6. The bars are held together by UV-activated glue, which also provides protection against buckling for each bar individually. The ensuing massive glass bar has a diameter of about 90 mm.

Special care is taken to avoid bending. The top detail is shaped like a rolling hinge. Pads of POM (Polyoxymethylene) provide elasticity and a uniform distribution of loads transported via steel shoes at the top and bottom of the glass column.

Side and front view of the glass column that would replace the existing concrete one.

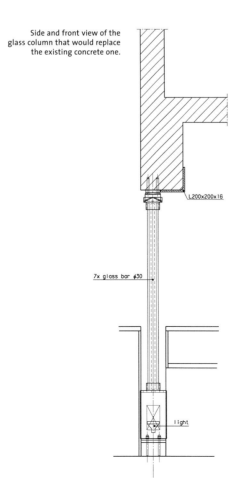

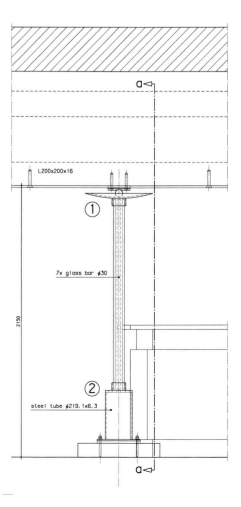

The perfect place for the glass column was marked by a concrete slab strategically positioned near the reception desk at the transition from the restaurant (where the conservatory of the old villa used to be) to the main building that is actually the volume of the former villa.

The column itself was no problem. The bundle concept was opted for; it was a coincidence indeed that I had made a contribution concerning this item to the British Institute of Engineers' publication *Structural Glass*. It represented a calculation model for this type of column, including a safety analysis of what would happen if some of the elements were to break.

The much more specific question was how to substitute a glass column for a concrete slab supporting a major part of the building.

It was decided, after installing temporary props, to reinforce the

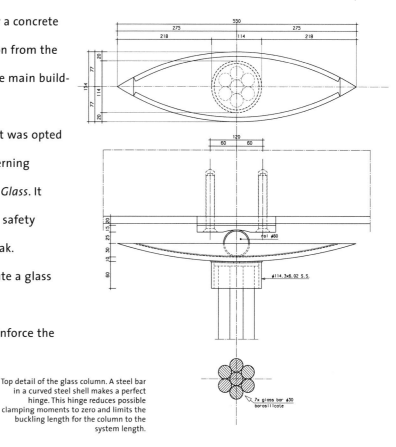

Top detail of the glass column. A steel bar in a curved steel shell makes a perfect hinge. This hinge reduces possible clamping moments to zero and limits the buckling length for the column to the system length.

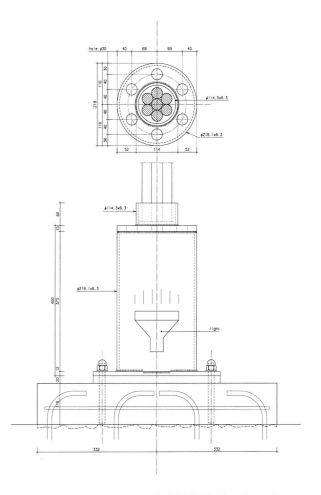

long concrete beam, which was exposed after removing the concrete slab, with an external steel construction. To this end steel profiles were anchored in the concrete with chemical cramps. The beam was now strong enough to handle the total span in an emergency, but the inherent bend would be considerable. Thus the glass column does indeed support the building, but should it fail for whatever reason, the coherence of the construction is warranted. By leaving the temporary support in place while the glass column was being built up and slowly turning it loose, with a hydraulic jack, load was added to the column. "Beauty is in the details," Mies van der Rohe once said, and my experience from working with many expert architects convinced me that what he said is very true. Therefore, the head and foot details were constructed with much care – since in these details lies the beauty of the glass column.

Foot detail of the glass column. The bundled glass stands on a neoprene pad with holes that allows light to shine through the column at night.

Glass Conservatory

Leiden, The Netherlands, 2001 – 2002

"New Technology Meets the Old City"

The owners of a big house at the Hooglandse Kerkgracht in the old town centre of Leiden decided to have their residence enlarged with a glass conservatory. Thus the view of their beautiful garden could be comfortably enjoyed in normal Dutch weather conditions (like rain, wind, cold, snow etc.).

The commission was given to the architectural office of B&D Architecten in Leiden; the project architect was Bas van Hille. Inspiration came from an all-glass conservatory in London, designed by Rick Mathers and engineered by the Dewhurst McFarlane office. I had the pleasure of looking at

Detail of façade, roof and connection of glass column to glass roof beam.

Connection detail (1) of glass roof panels to historic wall.

```
existing brickwork
15
12mm toughened
30                9 12 9
                     30
37        silicone joint on backfill
stainless steel U-profile
U30.30.30.2 RVS316
```

Cross section over glass roof beam. Glued connection (detail 2) of insulated roof panel to glass beam.

```
8
insulated glass 10-12-5.5x2pvb
                                        33
                                        6
2x PE backfill    structural silicone joint 7.5x6mm
glass beam 101010, resin layered
34
```

The connecting detail of the glass beam to the existing brick wall. By means of a gliding slot connection the glass beam is directly stable during assemblage.

this conservatory when I visited my colleague Tim McFarlane in London. A glued connection was required where the glass post meets the glass beam. This would be the first one of its kind to be constructed in the Netherlands. A Dutch firm from Schiedam, Van den Heuvel Glas, was given the commission to build the conservatory. A building permission was difficult to acquire in the historical centre of Leiden where, apart from the regular procedures, it was imperative to win approval from the surveyor of the monuments. Basically, it was not allowed to extend a house by a conservatory of this scale, but since this addition was to be constructed entirely of glass the surveying committee was tempted to make an exception and give it a try, a remarkable decision!

How does a glass beam meet a 350-year-old brick wall? We tried to detail this out in the most invisible way: the glass beam was to look as if

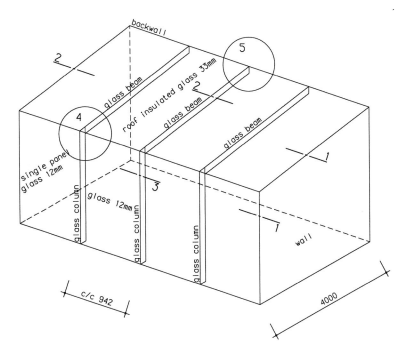

Overall drawing of all structural elements.

The area covered by the conservatory is 4.85 by 4.10 m. The height varies between
4.15 and 3.37 m. Basic part of the structure is the portal formed by
a glass post with a length of c. 3,300 mm and a glass beam with a
length of c. 4,200 mm. It was decided to make a stiff corner where
the beam meets the post. A UV-active glue had to be applied on
site to ensure this.

Both the beam and the post consist of three layers of float glass, each 10 mm
thick. The panels are glued to each other by resin instead of pvb-
foil. The roof panels were isolated ones: 10-12-5.5 pvb-glued. For
the façade one layer of toughened glass was chosen, 12 mm thick.

disappearing in the brick wall. The brick wall was constructed using the typical

17th-century method: it was about 300 mm thick and made of massive hard-

baked bricks. It was possible to carve a 110-mm-deep slot and bolt a stainless

steel U-profile into it. To this stainless steel shoe the glass beam was clamped.

The clamping device was considered to allow for tolerances and be able to follow

settlements which were to be expected from the new foundation. The remaining

part of the hole was filled with mortar. To make the surface of the wall as origi-

nal as possible on the outside, slices sawed from the removed original stones

were glued to the mortar.

It was decided to glue the connection between the post and the

roof beam on site although it might have been better done in the workshop

under controlled conditions. The choice for gluing on site was made by the

View of the roof of the London
conservatory.

Night view of the glass conservatory
in London. One day a thief fled over
the glass roof leaving his foot prints
behind. Did he (or she?) realize that it
was a glass roof?

contractor for reasons of measurement control. The plates were glued in such a way that the stiffest connection was achieved. In the London conservatory this was done by ending the top of the post with one inner panel of three going on and the two other stopping; the central panel of the beam stops and the two outer ones go on. Thus the two elements, post and beam, fit into each other. However, the remaining space between them, which has to be filled with glue, is out of control and varies considerably, leading to less control in the gluing process. Instead, we preferred to make the central panels of both post and beam continue and rest on each other. The glue is applied to the surface, then two separate panels are pressed against the side and the glue hardens.

It seems, however, that exceptional methods also attract exceptional problems. One glued connection failed and the portal had to be broken

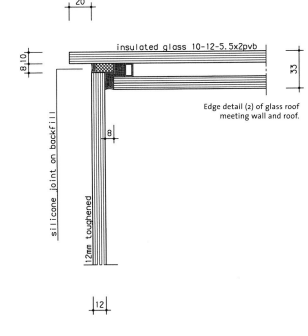

Edge detail (2) of glass roof meeting wall and roof.

Silicone glue was used for all connections and joints; even uplift forces were calculated to be taken up by these joints.
Transversal stability is provided by the frame action of the post and beam which are glued together, lateral stiffness is provided by the in-plain action of the roof and the façade. The silicone joint glued to the glass and the brick wall also provides waterproofing.

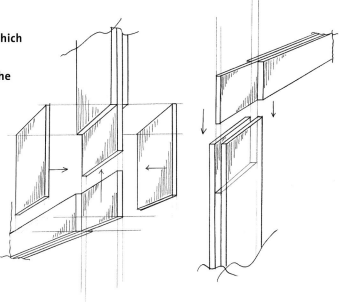

Two ways a laminated glass beam can be connected to a laminated glass-disc column. Left: the 'Leiden'-solution; right: the 'London'-solution.

The glass conservatory as a transparent extension to the old house.

resulting in an extra post and beam having to be ordered plus the waiting time involved. A glass lintel especially made to span the door opening broke after assembling, causing half the roof to sway unstably and forcing the workers to quickly remove two glass roof panels. The client despaired at this stage but eventually all problems were solved, and the newly created lovely "room" attached to the house could be enjoyed.

Supercolumn (Concept)

1996, not realized

"Water and Fishnet"

A supercolumn is a combination of three very different materials: water, glass and the so-called super-thread materials. Water and glass share two properties: they are both transparent and both capable of taking up huge compression forces. The supercolumn combines the best of both elements. Water is the best non-compressible material for the vertical bearing-part of a column. The water inside a glass cylinder transports the compression forces due to the load on top of the column. The glass cylinder in its turn keeps the water inside (waterproof!). The pressure of the water is taken up by a tensioned ring-action.

The Sabolovka Radio Tower in Moscow, 1919 – 1922, by the engineer Vladimir Suchov (1853 – 1939). Compared to the Eiffel Tower this type requires only about 25 % of the steel for the same performance; very limited deformation.

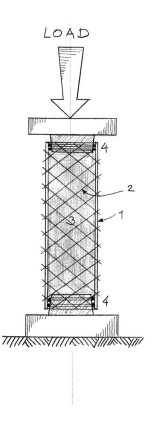

Supercolumn

1. Glass (hollow) column (cylinder-type).
2. Spiral-wiring of super-fibres in two opposite directions around the glass column.
3. Water.
4. Piston-like end-detail, water proof due to pressure on top.

Now tension in glass is not a preferable situation. This is where the third material comes in. The idea is to apply so-called super-thread materials like Twaron or Kevlar (polyaramids) as outside reinforcements to the glass cylinder. By winding these highly stress-resistant threads around the cylinder – in two opposite spirals in order to provide optimal cover – a major improvement to the structural capacity could be achieved. This concept of structural improvement by winding was worked out at the end of the 19th century by the brilliant Russian structural engineer Suchov. He made some beautiful large masts in the former USSR based on this principle. The spiralling threads would absorb the tensile ring-stresses caused by the immense vertical load. Thus such an unusual combination of glass, super-fibres and water would create a supercolumn.

GLASS FAÇADES

"Engineering is not a science.
 Science studies particular events to find general laws.
 Engineering design makes use of these laws to solve particular
 problems. In this it is, more closely related to art or craft;
 as in art, its problems are underdefined; there are many
 solutions, good, bad or indifferent ones.
 The art is, by a synthesis of ends and means, to arrive at a good
 solution. This is a creative activity, involving imagination,
 intuition and deliberate choice."

Ove Arup

Glass Façade for Educatorium Restaurant
Utrecht, The Netherlands, 1994 – 1997

Glass Façade for Natural Museum
Rotterdam, The Netherlands, 1997

Experimental School Façade
Heerlen, The Netherlands, 1994 – 1998

'Liberation' Carillon
The Hague, The Netherlands, 1994 – 1995

Rock-Stabilised Façade Design for EXPO 2000 Pavilion
Hanover, Germany, 1998

Façade Support Systems for University Libary
Utrecht, The Netherlands, 1997 – 2004

Glass-Walled House
Talus du Temple, Near Noyers/Avallon, France, 2000 – 2001

Casa da Musica
Porto, Portugal, 1998 – 2004

Façade detail of the Grand Palais
exhibition building in Lille, France, by
OMA. The fishscale-like overlapping
single glass panels make a lively
façade; getting this watertight is
another story …

A façade is a special type of wall. It separates inside from outside. The difference in position implies that this special type of wall has to satisfy substantial requirements in terms of building physics. Also the wind forces on façades, pulling at and pushing against them, as well as temperature-induced movement and water-tightness play an important role. These requirements make the designing and building of façades a difficult but challenging task – which, however, offers engineers the opportunity to devise appealing structures: "Every disadvantage has an advantage," to quote the famous Dutch soccer player Johan Cruijff.

Glass plays an essential role in the façade. By its property of transparency it opens up our buildings to the outside world. This psychological effect is very valuable. People may enjoy the view on the outside world and are not divided from it by a solid closed wall. Especially in the colder regions of this planet this is an essential aspect. Houses and offices can be kept comfortable much easier without having to give up the possibility of looking outside. But the introduction of glass into the façade has opened up the building not only from inside to outside but also from outside to inside. Certainly in modern architecture there is a tendency to open up buildings by using very large façades that are as transparent as possible. The visual borderline of what is in or outside the building becomes, on purpose, blurred. However, creating complete glass walls leads to new problems concerning the comfort inside the buildings. In winter, warmth passes easily through the glass façade, and in summer the heat of the sun is absorbed inside leading to excessive temperatures: the greenhouse effect.

Façade of new extension to the Musee des Beaux Arts in Lille, France. The façade of the old Museum is reflected in the mirroring glass.

A single glass panel is not a good insulator, warmth travels easily through it. The introduction of double glass was a major improvement. The closed-up small gap filled with air in between the two glass panels provides a good warmth insulation. Double glass improves the comfort in the building, avoids condensation in winter and reduces the amount of energy required to heat the building. Nowadays, double glazing is improved even more by filling the gap in the insulated panel not with air but with inert gases like argon and by vaporizing thin layers of precious metals on the glass surface. The rate of warmth insulation has been improved to a degree that a new danger is called up: in summer, the heat cannot go outside! Air-conditioning is no good solution to this problem. Architects and engineers need to be more critical of constructing façades automatically with insulated glass panels. Certain areas of a building, like entrance halls, can be seen as "half"-climate zones. In this chapter various examples are presented showing the range of possibilities for making glass façades.

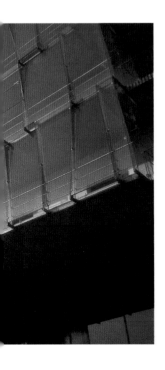

Glass Façade for Educatorium Restaurant

Utrecht, The Netherlands, 1994 – 1997

"Large Fins, Standard Detail"

The façade of the Educatorium restaurant varies in height from 3.50 to 8 m. To be more precise, we were not allowed to call it a façade, because in the view of the architects it is an open cross section of the building filled up with glass, offering passers-by, especially at night, a view of what is happening inside.

The design concept called for glass panels in maximum available sizes, in order to open up the canteen to the outside as much as possible. It was only logical to minimize at the same time the dimensions of the vertical steel mullions.

The insulated glass panels used for this façade have a maximum height of 6 m and consist of an inner blade of 2 x 6 mm annealed glass, a 10 mm cavity and an outer blade of 1 x 10 mm annealed glass. With their width of 1.80 m they adopt a rhythm that matches the building.

Exterior view.

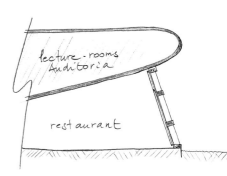

Glass facade Educatorium.
Plan of (part of) the ground level of Educatorium:

1. Restaurant area.
2. Kitchen area.
3. Entrance slope to the restaurant.
4. 8-m-high glass façade, here the stabilizing fins are on the outside.
5. Glass façade with the fins on the inside.

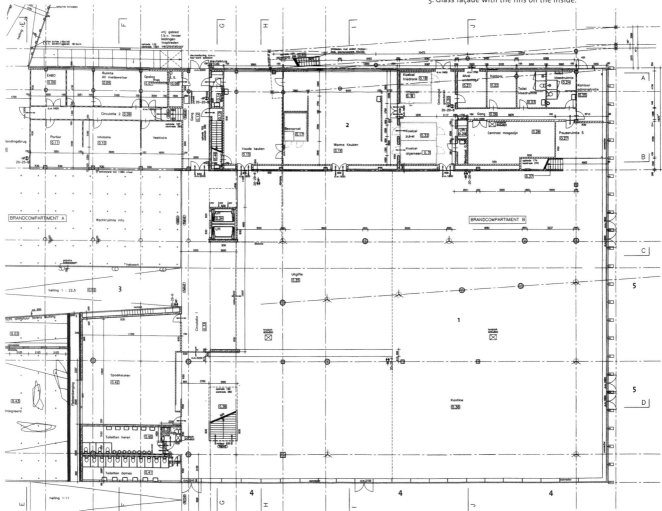

Therefore, in order to absorb the pressure and suction of the wind, glass fins were added to the vertical aluminium joints.

Much imagination and research resulted in a beautiful aluminium detail for a waterproof connection of glass panel and fin, which mitigated the visual impact of the aluminium profile. But then the problem arose that some of the fins had to be 8 m high while the maximum regular length of toughened glass available in the Netherlands was approximately 4.50 m. So a mechanical connection of the fin was inevitable. We succeeded in convincing the architects that in order to avoid creating a weak point this joint should not be in the centre of the span. Two connections were introduced instead, creating a distribution of 2 m – 4 m – 2 m which more or less matched the glass panel height of 6 m, so that the joints would form a pattern. Unfortunately, the most banal

In order to minimize vertical steel elements, glass fins were integrated into the vertical aluminium mullions. Calculation proved that 400-mm-deep fins, positioned at a distance of 2 m centre-to-centre and with a thickness of 15 mm would suffice. They needed to be made of toughened glass in order to allow for the holes needed for the steel bolts that attach the fins to the main structure. These connections are sliding on top and fixed at the bottom.
The necessary joints within the fins use a connection of two bolted stainless steel plates, transferring the friction forces between the steel/neoprene/glass surfaces, which are caused by the tightening of the bolts.

technical solution for the joint was opted for and my favourite version was not used, but I knew that one day its chance would come (see page 86 – 87).

A nice feature of the building design is that in the west façade the fins are set outside, while in the north facade they are positioned on the inside.

The (banal) two-clamping-steel-plates solution to connect two glass fin elements.

Interior view. A sea of light flows in from the 8-m-high glass façade.

Glass fin, façade Educatorium.

1. Stainless steel plates with bolts.
2. Neoprene pads between glass and steel.

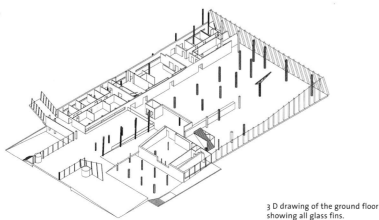

3 D drawing of the ground floor showing all glass fins.

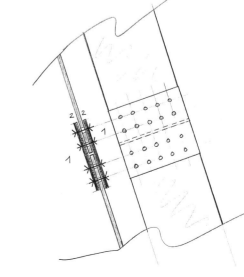

Glass Façade for Natural Museum

Rotterdam, The Netherlands, 1997

"Large Fins, Minimal Detail"

Outside view of the Natural Museum in Rotterdam. In the glass façade the glass fins take up the wind forces.

The sophisticated version of a glass fin joint that was developed but not selected for the Educatorium restaurant glass wall could be used very soon afterwards. The architect Erick van Egeraat asked for a maximum transparency façade for a new passage at the Natural Museum in Rotterdam. Again we used glass fins as stabilizing elements, which here had to be 6 m high, so that a single connection between the two sections of each fin was enough. Here stresses were not critical, so the connection could be made in the middle. This had the extra advantage that no shear force had to be transported but only

The floor-to-ceiling glass façade of 6 m height is stabilized by glass fins of the same height. The 6 m span is split into pieces of 4 m and 2 m.

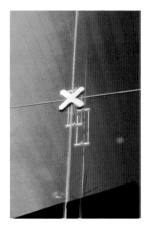

Exterior view of the structural connection, together with the elegant connection for the four insulating glass panels of the façade that meet here.

compression and tensile forces. The connection of the glass wall panel to the fin had to be made with a pointed fastener, however, as the architect preferred this type of connection. We invented a cross-shaped, or to put it more poetically, a butterfly-shaped fastener, mounted directly onto the glass fin. Together with the open quality of the panel-fin construction this results in a minimum use of steel and a maximum use of glass.

Personally I am very charmed by the technical detail of the connection of the glass fin, which was worked out by the contractor with much feeling for the material. Later I learnt that the architect had regretted the introduction of what he saw as a "dominant technical detail". It was, however, the first time that this "stitch-technique" connection between two glass parts had been carried out successfully. For me, the elegant "absence" of steel and the subdued

No-nonsense connection for two elements of a glass fin. As only bending moment has to be transported, no diagonals are required.

presence of the forces at work in this construction are two major aspects which make this a beautiful detail. But the eyes of an engineer do not see what the eyes of his colleague, the architect, might see, as Le Corbusier put it mildly.

The fins have a depth of 400 mm, they are made of 15 mm toughened glass and are positioned at a distance of 2.50 m from centre-to-centre. For the connection we used the "repairing-by-stitching" method, with steel cables for tensions and direct contact for pressures. The panels of the façade consist of one layer of 12-mm-thick toughened glass. The steel detail to hold the façade panels in its place is bolted directly to the glass fin.

Glass façade.

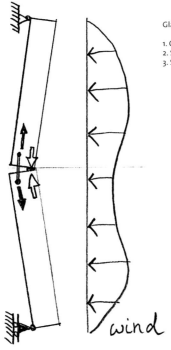

Glass fin, Natuur Museum Rotterdam.

1. Glued-in POM – plug in glass.
2. Steel H-profile with neoprene pads.
3. Steel ties with nuts.

wind

Experimental School Façade

Heerlen, The Netherlands, 1994 – 1998

"Web and Flange of Glass"

Interior view of the glass façade.

The façade, which is 13 m high, also carries the roof. The innovative steel/glass mullions are placed in a rhythm of 1.80 m centre-to-centre. The hollow steel section (150 x 150 mm) serving as mullion carries the roof and functions as attaching-point for the standard aluminium façade system. A web of 8-mm-thick toughened glass is attached to the steel profile.

All connections of the web to the steel hollow section, but also between the different glass elements of the web are by steel bolts, clamping the glass with an inner neoprene layer. At the joints of the web a stainless steel plate attaches the glass web panels but also supports the glass flange, which is made of 2 x 10 mm toughened glass.

There has been a tendency for some time in the policy of the Dutch Ministry of Education to integrate almost all kinds of higher education into very large buildings. In the case of Hogeschool Limburg, the range goes from nurse-training to a technical department for engineering, the latter being the reason why the brief called for the use of all kinds of structural materials, like steel, concrete and wood throughout the building.

Our suggestion to make an experimental glass structure appealed to the client. Budgets for this type of building are not large, and it is hard to make something special or original, but as we were the structural engineers for the entire building we succeeded in saving money on the major budget-consuming part of the program, the school classrooms, by using a very effecient structure there.

The object and location for the experimental glass structure, defined in cooperation with the architect, was a 13-m-high façade in a much-frequented corridor. A footbridge passes halfway up in front of the façade, adding to the appeal of the site for demonstration purposes. And the height of the façade would have needed structural attention anyway.

We set out to invent a small steel element intended to be toughened or stiffened by a glass fin-type of structure. This was inspired by the efficiency discovered in the 19th century when standard steel profiles were developed and industrially produced.

They combine minimum weight with maximum performance of the profile. Worked out in more detail, the idea turned into an adaptation of the H-steel-beam concept. The basis of this concept is to remove material where it

The connections of the plates forming the flange are provided by the "Zwitserleven" detail (see pages 32 – 35). All glass elements are, of course, laminated. The detailing of the actual façade was kept as standard as the rest of the building.

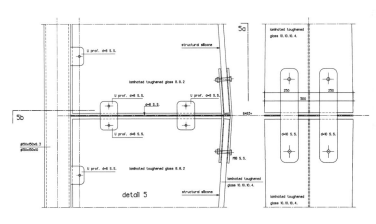

Connection of the two glass beams making a 2 m and a 4 m beam into one 6 m beam.

is not loaded or used otherwise and add material in places where there is maximum stress. The trick is to make the web as slender as possible and the flanges very thick. The creative process eventually resulted in a small steel hollow section combined with a thin web and broad flanges both made of glass, forming a parabola-shaped glass/steel mullion.

One intention was to expose the course of the bending moment exercised by the wind load in order to emphasize the structural aspects. We achieved this by giving the web a curved shape. The shape of the flanges is also curved in relation to the web. Wind pressure causes stress in the glass flanges, but at a low level so that it can be controlled. However, the pulling of the wind causes compression forces in the glass, so that the buckling behaviour turned out to require serious attention. The immense buckling length of 13 m, and the

View through the glass web of the façade towards the side of the glass flange.

Detail with the three basic elements: steel hollow section in the plane of the façade, glass web and glass flange.

fact that the façade also carries the roof, made the problem even more acute. It was solved by using the stiff plain of the façade as support and, in the direction perpendicular to the façade, by increasing the stiffness of the hollow section by reinforcing the wall of the hollow section. The ensuing combination of steel and glass is able to take up all forces exercised by the wind (push and pull) and to cope with the buckling summoned by the roof load.

A very transparent and surprisingly glittering facade was created, drawing the attention of all students interested in technology and related fields. Unfortunately, for reasons of climate control a sun-blocking grill was placed in front of the façade, made of big horizontal fins. On a sunny day this is no real problem, but on a somber, gloomy day the transparency we tried to achieve structurally by using glass is no longer noticeable.

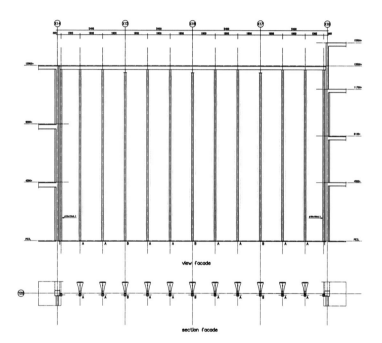

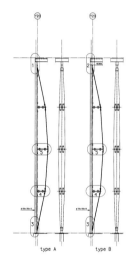

Front view.

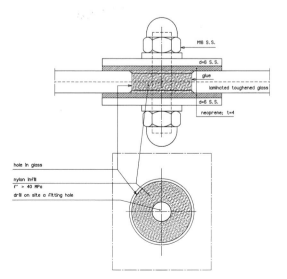

The beams are tapered so as to illustrate the diminishing bending moment.

Technical detail of the connection of two glass elements in the flanges and the web of the Heerlen glass beam.

The most important achievement of this façade remains the fact that it was possible to use steel in order to transfer our structural knowledge to glass.

'Liberation' Carillon

The Hague, The Netherlands, 1994 – 1995

"Glass Echo Pit"

In commemoration of the liberation of the Netherlands from German Nazi occupation by the Allied Forces in 1945, a committee representing all layers of the Dutch political scene was appointed to decide on the erection of a monument. After a very thorough selection process, the decision was taken to ask the architect Ben van Berkel to design a modern version of a carillon, an instrument that in medieval times had a marked presence in European cities and added to their liveliness. In a carillon many, even rather big bells are played together, preferably in harmony. The size of the bells and their impressive

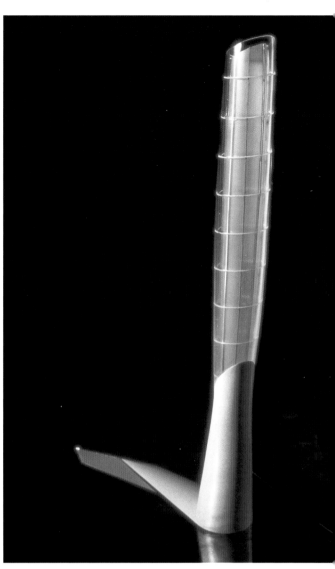

Model. From the water rises a polished concrete foot holding a glazed glass tube that reflects the music of the carillon.

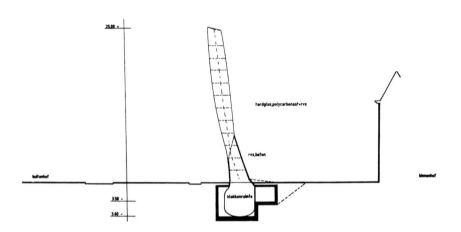

Cross section of the Carillon, situated in the Hofvijver (Pond) in The Hague, directly opposite the Dutch Parliament.

volumes implied that they were usually placed in the bell towers of churches. Every quarter of an hour they played a cheerful tune to mark the time, thus adding a musical dimension to city life.

The carillon was to be located in the pond, the "Hofvijver", directly beside the medieval buildings of the Dutch Parliament. Ben van Berkel took his commission very seriously and made a beautiful design for a carillon in a submerged concrete cellar, with the sounds of the bells coming out of a glass tower which was to rise mysteriously from the water. It would have been the perfect marriage between a modern design and the medieval concept of a carillon.

ABT developed the structure and the foundation for the project. After some scrimmages the funding was established, so life at first looked sweet and sunny for this project. However, there are other committees which have the duty to preserve the quality of the historical city of The Hague. They often have such a straightforward concept of their task that they object to almost anything which might look modern. They prefer things the way they are and standstill is their supreme goal. The idea of a modern glass tower emerging from the Hofvijver was their worst nightmare come true.

Showing their amiable side they proposed another site, also near the Parliament at the crossing of two important streets. Time was running short, and when even the guild of players of historic carillons started to remark on possible problems of the sound produced by an underground carillon the organizing committee cancelled the project. A wasted chance to let the world see that medieval cities can absorb mild quantities of modern architecture and become even more beautiful.

The foundation was to be a concrete cellar cast on site resting on piles. A steel frame of tubes, round 150 mm, mounted on this concrete structure carries curved glass panels of 10 mm toughened glass. The curving of the glass was to be done with the help of a set of specially made moulds, thus combining the process of curving with the process of toughening the glass.

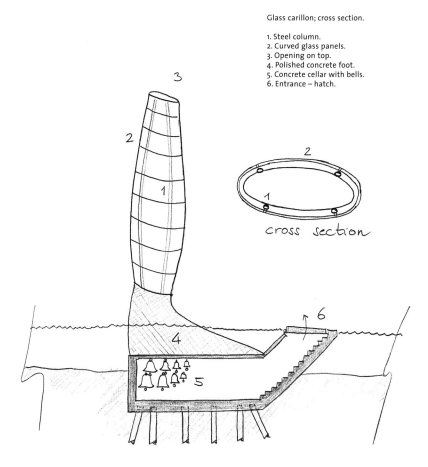

Glass carillon; cross section.

1. Steel column.
2. Curved glass panels.
3. Opening on top.
4. Polished concrete foot.
5. Concrete cellar with bells.
6. Entrance – hatch.

cross section

Rock-Stabilized Façade Design for EXPO 2000 Pavilion

Hanover, Germany, 1998

"Rock-and-Roll Engineering"

In the very first design stage of the Dutch pavilion for the EXPO 2000 (see also pages 154–155) severe budget cuts had to be made. Thus the Oyster, the space foreseen for showing films, with its ferroconcrete imitation of an external calcium skeleton was cancelled because it was too expensive. Instead an additional room was created for this purpose, situated directly below the top of the pavilion. The design called for a transparent façade there, in order to maintain the principle of transparency applied to the pavilion. But obviously, when a film is shown the room must be dark. How to bring this about? It was

The effect of the hanging rock is structurally that of a stiffening spring. As the mullions of the glass wall start to deform due to the wind the rock will be pushed horizontally.
By its pendulum effect, which acts like a support, gravity starts to push back by a force W (= weight rock) multiplied by sinus (angle) (= slope of pendulum axis). Hence the weight of the rock can be calculated considering the allowable horizontal movement.

Top part of Dutch pavilion.

1. Stabilising rock.
2. Double glass wall.
3. Double glass wall filled with ink.
4. Steel cable tensioning fabric in façade (water wall).
5. Waterfilm on fabric, water "overflows" from "lake" at the pavilion.

suggested to build a double wall with a cavity of a few centimeters, which would be quickly filled with pitch-black ink when a film was about to start. Another alternative were heavy lightproof curtains running in the cavity. Anyway, the next question was how to construct such a double glass wall without exceeding the budget. The planned height of 6 m did not cause any particular problems, but as the maximum thickness for glass panels is 19 mm due to production limitations, the combination of these dimensions with the wind forces at this level above ground would create internal stresses and deformation to such extent that a support was required in the middle.

One of the paradoxes of human existence is that you can fight something with its opposite – thus hatred is cured with love and poverty with wealth, and vice versa. In our banal problem something vulnerable like a glass

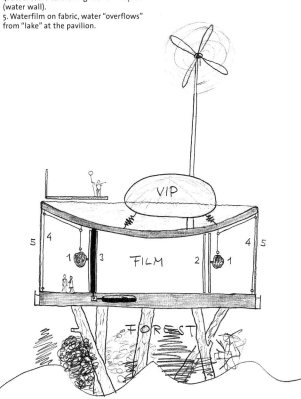

panel, which was too light, had to be compensated by something heavy: for instance a rock. This is the scenario: Halfway up the floor height, a heavy rock hangs in front of the outside of the glass wall, which is attached to it. When the wall gets beaten by a gust of wind, the panel bends and starts pushing against the rock. This kind of support will reduce the tension in the glass by a factor $1^2/0.251^2$ (meaning to the power of 2), a factor four. Bending is even reduced by a factor 16! The energy exercised by the gust of wind on the panel will be translated into a movement of the rock, whose mass and inertia will absorb and cushion it. When the gust of wind dies down the rock will return to its original position, like a pendulum.

What is more, it would be a multifunctional rock: all kinds of sound and light equipment would be integrated, a feature that particularly appealed to

Experimental test of a rock-stabilized glass panel in the ABT office.

All steel or aluminium members of the façade can be calculated for spanning not from bottom floor slab to top floor slab, but only from support to support, with the rock forming a support.

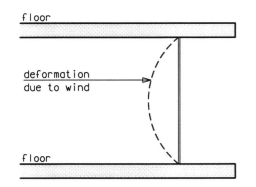

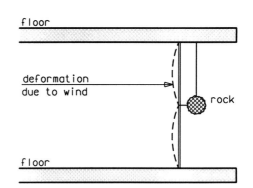

Diagrams showing the positive effect of rock stabilization on a high façade.

the architects, and last but not least the weight of the rock was used for stretching the rain curtain along the façade.

Of course, this was too good to be true and the plan met an inglorious end in another, rather hectic, attempt to cut the budget. Eventually, the glass façade was replaced by closed walls. Yet this idea is too good to die anonymously, and that is why this publication is an attempt to challenge people to make this poetical image come alive. It would mean the start of – rock-and-roll engineering.

Façade Support Systems for University Library

Utrecht, The Netherlands, 1997 – 2004

"Choose Your Rock"

This project is another item of the new building for the University Library in Utrecht (see page 68). In certain parts of the building (see computer image) 25-m-high glass façades had to withstand the force of the wind. We worked out a great number of possible solutions. Wiel Arets first decided in favour of the "floating rocks " solution (see pages 93 – 94) but later changed his mind to the "tensioned cable" solution.

The "tensioned cable" solution is based on the principle of absorbing horizontal forces by a pre-stressed cable that stiffens in the process. It is

Three proposals for libary façade in Utrecht.

A. Two hanging rocks.
a. The resulting static scheme.
B. One hanging rock.
b. The resulting static scheme.
C. Tensioned cable.
c. The resulting static scheme.

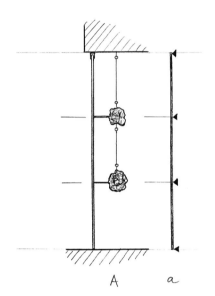

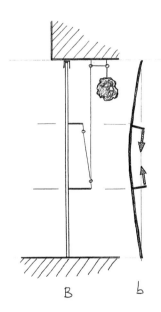

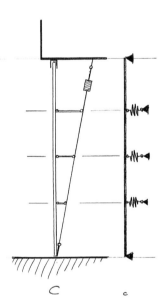

A   a   B   b   C   c

also based on the natural phenomenon that wind pressure on a façade area is about twice as intense as the pulling action of the wind. Thus we can vary the cross section areas of a wind-load-carrying element according to the forces which have to be absorbed.

Whether this façade will be constructed in this way is, at the time of writing, still hidden in the future.

Computer generated image. The three systems described above where designed for the high glass façades.

Glass-Walled House

Talus du Temple – Near Noyers /Avallon, France, 2000 – 2001

"Roofs Can Float!"

Setting and scenery play a major part for this project. A Dutchman had acquired a small farmhouse at the edge of an estate on the banks of the river Serein in central France, some 100 km south of Paris. Near the border of this estate the Duchess of Nassau had built a *temple d'amour* in the 18th century: a small tea pavilion for, one may only guess, romantic encounters which had to be kept out of the direct sight from the castle. But time rolls on and the duchesses disappeared. The temple, however, remained and was joined in the 19th century by a railway for which a bridge was built to cross the Serein River. In the 20th

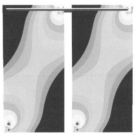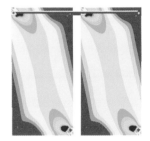

Two finite-element-method computer images showing possible worst cases for the stabilizing glass walls, one with a tensile diagonal in the glass, the other with a compression diagonal. If these constructions succeed, all intermediate stress distribution can be handled as well.

Lookout room on top of the old railway landing, in autumn.

century the railway was dismantled and only the two natural stone landings of

the bridge were left standing. The Dutchman's house stood near this landing

from the top of which one had a nice view of the river and the country. When it

was discovered that inside the landing was a so-called gunpowder room used in

time of war to blow up the bridge, it was decided to make use of this outlook

and build a room, and a shelter on top of the landing.

Architect Dirk Jan Postel was asked to make a design for this

project. Inspired by the beautiful 360° view, he opted for glass walls all around

that should carry the roof. He and I had discussed possibilities of such a concept

earlier. Since there was no active interference of the authorities, we were able

to realize this rather challenging structure. We calculated in a spatial finite-

element-model that glass panels could not only carry the weight of the roof

**The room measures 5,040 by 5,100 mm. The internal height is 2,30 m. The walls
are made of laminated toughened glass panels, 2 x 10 mm thick.
The fixed parts are connected by bolts to a steel angle mounted on
the ground/top of the landing or on the roof. In the front and back
façade hinged glass doors are installed. The roof is a wooden box
clad by copper plates.**

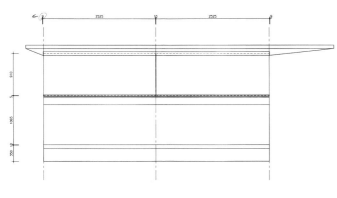

Side elevation.

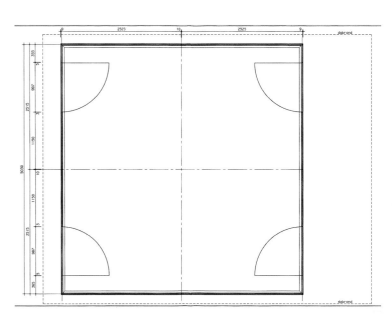

Plan.

Interior, showing the hatch/opening
through which the former
gunpowder room, now guest room,
can be reached.

but also provide stability for the structure. For this purpose bolts connected the fixed parts of the walls to the rest of the structure. The Alverre firm was asked to make and mount the glass, which they did in three days. The wooden, copper-clad roof was prefabricated on the ground below, then lifted over the freestanding glass walls and slowly lowered onto them.

The view from the top of the landing is amazing, and especially at night the roof seems to float in the air. Since completion in May 2001 two serious storms have gone over the area. The structure withstood the wind gusts perfectly. Only later I learned that a similar concept was realized, on a larger scale, in Rheinbach in Germany. It is interesting to see how practical Dutch engineering is worked out in comparison to German scientific engineering.

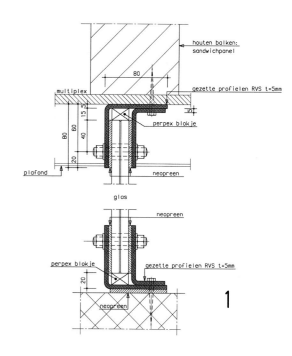

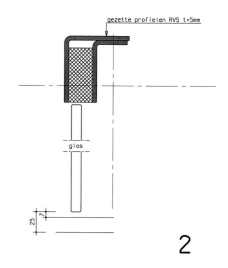

Front elevation.

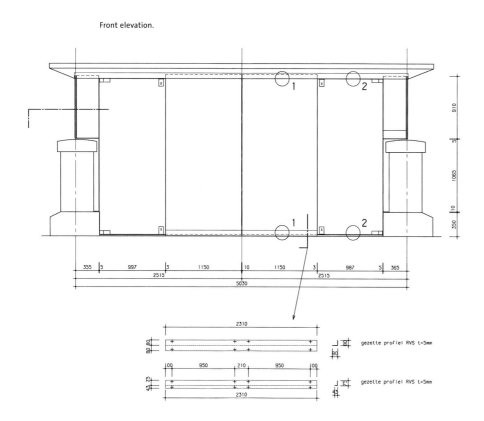

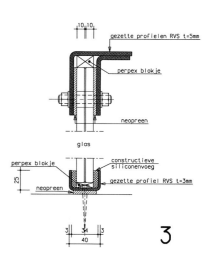

Details 1–3.

Both buildings, however, give evidence to the fact that the
architectural practice has been expanded by the possibility of surrounding glass
walls on which the roof seems to float. This project won the Benedictus Award
2002 for outstanding innovations in laminated glass.

View from the terrace showing in the
background the 18th-century *temple d'amour*.

Side elevation of the old railway-
bridge landing with the glass-walled
house on top.

Nightscape, showing perfectly the effect of the floating roof.

Casa da Musica

Porto, Portugal, 1998 – 2004

"Waves on the Window"

View of the real Casa da Musica during construction, April 2003. The biggest window to be filled with corrugated glass is right in front.

In 2001 Rotterdam and Porto were Cultural Capitals of Europe. Both are characteristic harbours. One is old and very cultural, boarding the Oporto River in the Porto wine area, its name meaning port itself. The other is new and very large, its name referring to a dyke (dam) in a small river, the Rotte. To celebrate this once-in-a-lifetime-event for a city, the people of Porto decided to build a new theatre as a central place for the activities.

This theatre can be seen as the counterpart of the structure of the glass dome in Rotterdam (see pages 136 – 137). The Office of Metropolitan

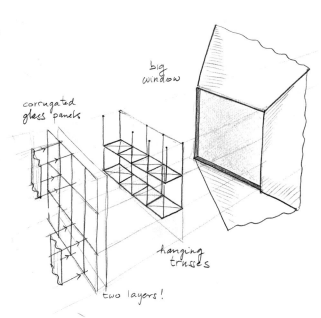

Sketch of the load-bearing system for the large windows, measuring 25 x 15 m.

The three very large windows measure c. 22 x 15 m, 14 x 9 m and 22 x 12 m. The corrugated glass panels measure c. 1.20 x 4.50 m. To incorporate an escape route in the structure and to cope with required acoustical insulation there is a double wall system: the corrugated glass on the outer wall is 10.10.2, two layers of 10-mm-thick clear glass; the inner wall is made out of 6.6.2, two layers of 6-mm-thick clear glass. The corrugated glass panels are mounted in specially made aluminium profiles making a watertight connection.

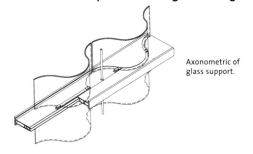

Axonometric of glass support.

Architecture (OMA), headed by the Dutch architect Rem Koolhaas, won the Porto theatre competition. The architect described the winning design as a white sculpted jewel placed on the steep banks of the river. The shape of the building is defined by the various rooms and circulation areas. It is to be made out of the white concrete for which Portugal is famous. The structural engineers were Ove Arup, London, in association with the local engineer AFA from Porto. ABT gave some advice on the concrete skin and worked out the structure for three large windows, together with the French consultant Robert Jan van Santen of Van Santen & Associés from Lille.

These three windows are large indeed, the biggest one measures 22 x 14.7 m. They are strategically placed, allowing a spectacular view over the city and its surroundings. To lend them more architectural importance the

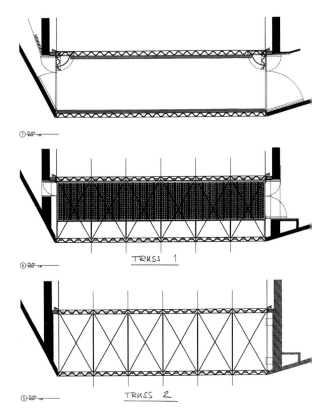

Section and plans of the structural wind trusses, with the walkway on top of one of them.

architect selected corrugated glass panels. This special type of glass is a new development, created by innovative workshops like the Cricursa firm in Barcelona, Spain. The largest sizes which could be made were about 5 x 1.2 m. This meant that a supporting structure was needed, especially because of the weight and the wind load, which can be rather high in the vicinity of the Atlantic Ocean. But architects see windows always as transparent and hate visible structures for blocking this concept. So we worked out a structure hanging from the roof, in order to have only tensile forces in dead load. To cope with the wind, we placed horizontal trusses with X-shaped diagonals in an interval corresponding to the production-size limitations. Then the need for an escape way crossing in front of one window brought the architect to the idea of using the horizontal trusses for this purpose. This made the life of the structural engineers a little harder.

For wind loads, trusses are placed at the position of each horizontal joint in the façade. On one location this truss is also used as an escape route. In order to hold the load of people fleeing over it, hangers to the concrete structure above connect various points of this truss.

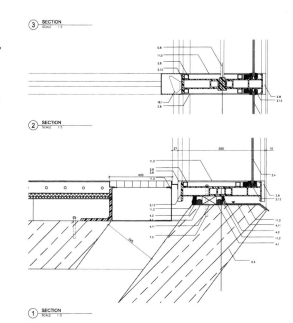

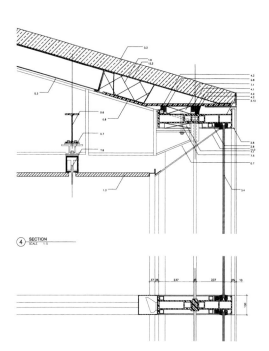

Top and bottom details of the large windows.

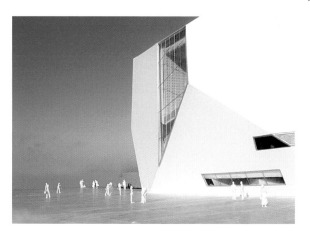

A model shows what the "white jewelbox with big windows" of the Casa da Musica will look like.

The required acoustic insulation was another issue. Two panels/ façades of glass had to be made, creating a void which was walkable and fire-resistant, the fire integrity demand being 30 minutes. Robert Jan van Santen worked out the very ingenious details of this façade with a little help from ABT. We worked out the wind trusses. The building was not finished in time to celebrate the 2001 Cultural Capital of Europe (with, however, a theatrical event on site in December), and at the time of writing it is slowly coming above ground level.

Architectural model. The black parts in the façades mark the various windows/openings in the white concrete skin.

A corrugated glass panel in the factory.

OTHER GLASS WALLS

"Don't fight forces, use them!"

R. Buckminster Fuller
(in: *Shelter*, 5, 1932)

The Artis Aquarium Dutch canal scenery.
We look into the underwater world at 1 m
below a Dutch canal.

Glass Wall for Educatorium Auditorium
Utrecht, The Netherlands, 1994 – 1997

Glass Houses
R.O.A.M., **Leerdam, The Netherlands, 1996**
House by Kruunenberg/van der Erven, Leerdam,
The Netherlands, 1996 – 2001

Aquarium Tank Glass Walls at Artis Zoo
Amsterdam, The Netherlands, 1995 – 1996

Acrylic Aquarium Tank Walls
Arnhem, The Netherlands, 1998 – 2001

Waterwall Concept for Eco-House
Diest, Belgium, 1998

Retaining Wall Concept – Transparent Dyke Concept
1997

Flexible Dyke-Top Concept
Deventer, The Netherlands, 1999

Glass Windshields
Nijmegen, The Netherlands, 1998

Walls separate areas in a very physical way. The material glass offers the possibility of creating a real physical separation between two spaces while at the same time allowing full insight into what happens beyond. In principle, walls occur in two different situations: inside buildings they chiefly serve acoustical and optical requirements. As part of the façade they protect the inside of the building from the outside climate.

Regarding the structural aspects a wall is just a special type of column. It is only far more wider than thick. Therefore, the remarks we made concerning columns could be repeated here. Instead we will concentrate on the question of how glass walls may be designed. Basically, we are following in the footsteps of the builders of gothic cathedrals. For the glory of God, they sought to make the walls of their churches as transparent as possible. They were only familiar with blockwork walls with windows in it, but with these materials they achieved almost immaterial walls with colourful stained-glass windows. The invention of the kinked high-rise arch, the flying buttress and the pier buttress led to enormous heights. Starting in the beginning with a maximum height of 15 m, in Beauvais (1245) they reached the enormous height of 48 m.

But Beauvais marked the end of this development: in 1284, during a heavy storm, the straight parts of the vaults collapsed. It is amazing that those light-weighted structures were built in a time when there was no theoretical understanding of how arches or beams or plates work and no computer programs existed which were able to deal with such spatially complicated structures. People then simply used their common sense, they learned from failures (which we do not see any more because only the successful solutions have survived) and tried each new time to make things a little higher and a little smaller.

Today that method of working is no longer acceptable. Most of all we have to erect safe structures; collapses must not occur. Fortunately, we now have a sound theoretical knowledge about structures and we do have the computers that can calculate the stresses and deformations of very complicated spatial structures.

In the next chapters we will concentrate on walls made of glass. For safety reasons we always use laminated glass for structural elements. The critical collapse criteria for a wall will be buckling or plying. Therefore, a glass wall must have a considerable thickness and hence quite a few layers. We could improve on this aspect by making a corrugated wall, but this type of glass has only recently become available (see pages 127 – 129). Another critical point is how to get the loads from the structure resting on top of the glass wall into the glass wall without causing too much concentrated stresses. The support should be as centralized as possible. Also the detail at the bottom of the wall, where the forces have to go into the foundation, has to be designed with these starting-points in mind.

Glass façades have been discussed in the previous part of this book. In this chapter we are looking at a variety of other kinds of glass walls, including earth-retaining walls.

Glass house, Leerdam. A glass wall
connects the spaces visually.

Glass Wall for Educatorium Auditorium

Utrecht, The Netherlands, 1994 – 1997

"A Wall with a Moving Window"

Examining a mock-up of the original structural design of the glass wall.

Part of the mock-up of the first glass wall design. Two tensioned steel cables separated by horizontal steel bars hold the glass panels.

The design concept for the Educatorium (see also pages 49 – 51, 84 – 85 and 142 – 147) was based on circulation needs. With a restaurant for 1,000 people, two lecture rooms for 400 and 500 people, and three examination halls seating 750 people, masses of students would move through the building on their way to examinations, attending a lecture or just having a meal or a coffee. The design idea was that of an inclined concrete floor slowly rising, then suddenly turning into a wall and immediately turning back over your head, forming a roof. A few façades were required to complement this flowing movement.

This glass wall, which varies in height from about 8 to 2.5 m, serves not only as separation but is also for acoustic insulation. Therefore, it is made from two layers of glass panels. The panels are 1.20 by 1.20 m and have a thickness of 8 mm. The glass is toughened.

The first structure of the C-500 glass wall.

1. Attachments (spring action, tensioning).
2. Steel cable (to be tensioned).
3. Steel bars as separators.
4. Central fixture to glass panel.
5. Glass panel.

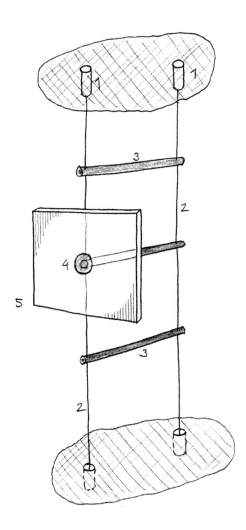

The north side of the building overlooks a rather wild, yet park-like landscape. Adequately, the design called for a glass façade for the lecture rooms on the first floor. Since the rooms are facing north, large glass surfaces are not a problem, as there is no danger of heating-up by the sun's radiation. But the client, the University, protested; lectures would demand a great deal of concentration, and it would be unacceptable to allow students to be diverted by the scenery. Furthermore, the required projection screen for presentations also called for a closed wall.

Obviously, there was a conflict of interest that was hard to solve without neglecting either of the two parties involved. All kinds of alternative proposals, like translucent glass walls with curtains, were studied, but no suitable solution was found. Then a representative of the Japanese Asahi Glass company visited OMA and presented a new type of glass, called Lumisty, which fascinated the architects. It has the surprising property of being entirely transparent like normal glass when looked at perpendicularly but translucent and greyish when looked at under an angle. This dual quality is created by a so-called holographic foil, glued invisibly onto the surface of the glass. Here was the solution the architects had been looking for: a limited view to respect the wish of the client, but also the possibility to create a little diversion for the students by opening a small window to the park. The new technology even made the façade respond better to the overall design concept of the building based, as described above, on circulation: People passing the lecture rooms encounter a window with the very surprising feature that it moves along with them on their way!

Each panel is supported by only one bolted connection in the centre to a steel tube round 46 mm. To give resistance against horizontal forces the two tubes, placed at a distance of about 300 mm from each other, are connected by massive glass bars round 30 mm. In this way they form a so-called ladder-frame that is capable of mobilizing two tubes into bending when one side of the wall is pushed. The frame hangs on the roof, allowing for deformation of the floor due to circulation.

Minimalized connection detail of glass bar and steel tubes in the ladder frame.

A problem that remained to be solved was to make the structure of the wall as "non-present" as possible. Our point of reference was the wonderful wall in the Kempinski Hotel at Munich Airport of 1993/94, where architect Helmut Jahn and structural engineer Jörg Schlaich had devised a concept of tensioned cables from floor to ceiling to which the glass panels forming the wall were attached. We adopted this brilliant idea but had to make a double wall for sound insulation, protecting the lecture room from sounds coming from the corridor. As a result there are two sets of cables and two separate layers of glass. In this way the problem of the varying height of the lecture room was tackled as well, by making the cables longer or shorter in relation to the slope of the floor. The tempered glass panels were clamped to the cable system in the centre of the panel, so that it was possible to use only one hole, one connection per panel.

As the glass wall had to follow a more or less circular curve, the straight panels overlap like the scales of a fish.

The wall was worked out in detail for the tender documents. There were no particular comments on the special structure during this tendering stage, but when the time came to realize the structure, the contractor declared this wall to be unbuildable. They agreed to make a mock-up on site, but its quality proved so poor for the client who eventually asked the design team to come up with an alternative.

In this situation I fell back upon the glass truss for the Zwitser-leven project (see pages 32 – 35). We developed a so-called ladder-frame – two vertical tubes connected by horizontal bars – and proposed glass bars similar to those of the truss used in the Zwitserleven project for the horizontal bars.

The effect of the Lumisty foil: looking straight at the panel means transparency, more oblique angles of view make the panel translucent.

The curving of the wall is achieved by making the glass panels overlap like the scales of a fish. This subtle detail provides maximum tolerances for the joints of the wall. Simple silicone joints make the wall soundproof.

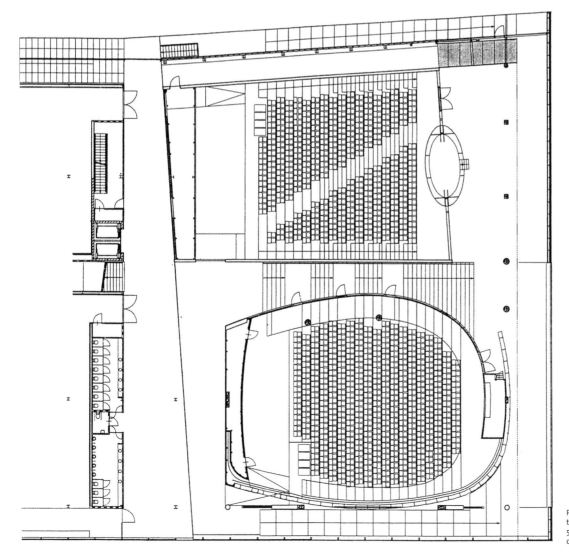

Plan of the two large auditoriums of the Educatorium, the one with 400 seats on top and the one with 500 seats below. The glass wall described here is the curved one of the 500-seat auditorium.

Interior of the glass wall. The ladder-frame
is composed of two vertical steel tubes
and glass bars as horizontal connections.

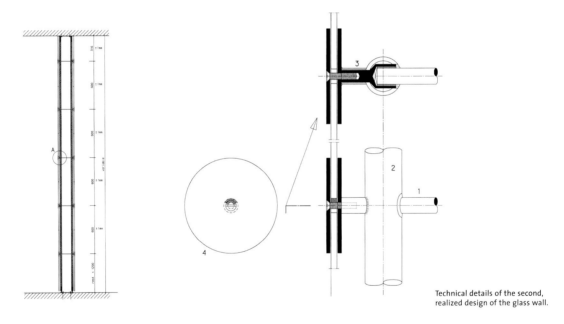

Technical details of the second,
realized design of the glass wall.

Thorough testing confirmed the approach. Unfortunately, the "invisible" detail
connecting the glass bars with the steel tubes was much affected by the heavy
use of silicone that was needed to cover up all the imperfections of this wall. The
overall effect, however, is still very impressive.

Exterior of the curved glass wall. The
structural truss going through the wall
creates interesting details.

Glass Houses

R.O.A.M., Leerdam, The Netherlands, 1996

House by Kruunenberg / van der Erven, Leerdam, The Netherlands, 1996 – 2001

R.O.A.M.: "Structural Glass Walls"

Leerdam, a small town near Rotterdam in the so-called Green Heart of Holland, is well known for its glass industry, mostly drinking glasses, vases and art objects. To emphasize this "glass connection" the local social housing foundation organized an architectural competition for a glass house on a site close to the town centre. Two young architects, Robert Winkel and Marco Henssen, contacted me, and the discussion resulted in the decision to use glass for the main building structure.

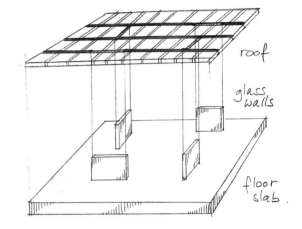

Technical sketch of the connection detail of structural glass wall and roof structure.

Resting on a concrete foundation slab on piles, four glass panels of 2.50 x 2.50 m toughened glass (thick 6 x 15 mm = 90 mm) carry steel beams and a wooden roof. The four glass walls also provide stability and take up the horizontal forces evoked by the wind.
The other glass walls are secondary elements and span from floor to roof to take up the wind loads.

The architectural concept of layered spaces led to the remarkable idea that glass walls were to constitute the building's primary structure. The outer spatial layer, along the façade of single glass, is a multi-functional half-climate zone: here plants can be kept, a first buffer against the winter cold or the summer heat is provided, traffic noise is reduced, and a visual block in this zone protects the privacy of the dwellers. The second zone – the living area –, separated from the façade zone by cupboards and screens, is the actual house. Finally, in the central part of the building, a translucent core houses the bathroom area.

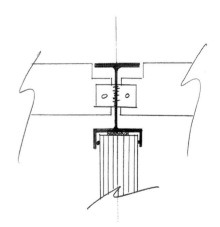

The main building structure consists of four huge laminated glass panels of about 2.50 x 2.50 m carrying steel beams and the wooden roof. The first idea for these glass panels, which function like columns, originated from

Family living in the R.O.A.M. glass house.

Nightscape of the R.O.A.M. glass house model.

the Artis Aquarium (see page 112) where I wondered whether the immense panels used there could also carry an important vertical load.

The design was not successful in the competition but remains noteworthy for its consistent integration of structures and functions.

The corridor of the glass house in Leerdam.
Glass surrounds the occupants on all sides, a mesmerizing
greenish glow radiates through the thick glass walls.

House by van der Erven/Kruunenberg: "A Glass Body"

The winning competition design by Van der Erven/Kruunenberg presented the surprising idea of a house with an entire laminated-glass body. (Later we learned that in a Japanese competition the same idea had been conceived independently.) I was asked to help building the house. Many problems including the question of comfort and privacy were involved. One question was how to glue large glass panels to this grotto-like shape. It seemed easiest to produce the largest possible sections in the workshop, under controlled conditions, and assemble them on site. Simple silicone oil was used as glue, as it keeps out the moisture and prevents the natural growth of algae in narrow spaces. Our involvement ended after a preliminary design.

Exterior of the Leerdam glass house.

Again based on a concrete floor and foundation, almost 80 m² of glass form the massive walls of this glass house. They consist of about 10,000 plates of glass, each 10 mm thick, stacked against each other by using the adhesive force called up by a very narrow crevice filled with a two-component silicone oil. The glass walls, which have a variable diameter of 200 to 600 mm, carry a wooden roof with big glass parts in it.

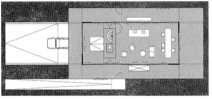

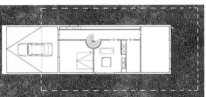
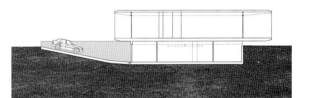

Plans and cross sections of the Leerdam glass house.

Glass house, Leerdam. An opening in the structural glass wall reveals its construction; small panels of glass are glued together.

Integration of standard glass windows into the system of thick structural glass walls.

Aquarium Tank Glass Walls at Artis Zoo

Amsterdam, The Netherlands, 1995 – 1996

"Let the Water Do the Job"

The renovation of the almost 100-year-old Artis Aquarium building required new aquariums and implied the construction of large glass panels resisting the pressure of 3 m of water. The idea was to make the glass panels take up this water load of 3,000 kg/m² – without mullions but with the help of floor-to-roof spanning.

It was a quite ambitious design in the eyes of the glass industry. Despite my point that glass, when protected by glass plates "taking the brunt", cannot be scratched or infested by the water, they ordered 6 layers of 15 mm

Aquarium showing a coral reef coastal zone. On the right the "self"-closing joint between the glass panels.

There are two types of aquarium, of which there are two of each . One type is filled up to a height of 1.20 m, with 3 x 15 mm toughened glass spanning from floor to floor. These aquariums allow a view into a canal in Amsterdam and into the beach zone of an artificial tropical coral reef. The other type presents a 3-m-high view into the deeper part of the coral reef and a similar view into a flooded Amazon forest. These panels – 6 x 15 mm – have to carry up to 3.5 m of water pressure. They are supported at the vertical seams by steel mullions, tubes 100 x 100 mm. All panels have a width of 1.75 m.

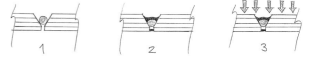

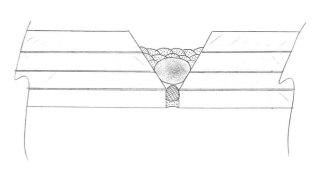

toughened glass where 3 x 15 mm with two protective glass layers of 5 mm would have been sufficient. The fortunate turn in this was that the immense panel later inspired the use of glass for a stability wall in the glass house competition (see pages 108 – 111).

The real beauty of the design lies, once more, in the details. For the connections of the mullion-free row of glass panels we developed a side detail with inclined edges. This inclination causes the soft neoprene tube in the joint to automatically close the opening when pressed by the water. Extra silicone joints added additional safety. So water pressure leads to waterproofing!

The Artis Aquarium detail.

1. Soft neoprene bar laid in v-shaped joint.
2. Silicone applied on both sides.
3. The water pressure pushes against the soft.
neoprene bar and provides perfect fitting (closure).

Acrylic Aquarium Tank Walls

Arnhem, The Netherlands, 1998 – 2001

"Glass is Not Always the Best Choice"

Although this is a book about glass structures, this does not imply that glass is the ideal solution for all situations requiring transparency. Today, many aquariums all over the world have large "panes" made of acrylic – basically polyacrylic or, if a better quality is required, polycarbonate. Glass is much stronger, much stiffer and much more durable; but in its endless wisdom the glass industry has decided to produce in its gigantic, permanently operating furnaces only glass in standard sizes and thicknesses. Any European client who wants to buy a 7-m-long pane may beg and plead, but will not see his wish

The large, 20 x 5 m window of the Arnhem Burgers Ocean aquarium tank. It is made of 400-mm-thick acrylic panels welded together on site to make one continuous plate with almost invisible seams.

fulfilled. Polyacrylate and polycarbonate are made by more flexible factories, and panels can be welded together in a fairly simple and almost invisible way, creating the illusion of looking through one big slab.

The clever structural engineer will use this soft material in a curved construction in order to achieve arch-like behaviour, which causes compression in the material. With a thickness of up to c. 400 mm such a transparent wall can resist 4 to 5 m of water pressure.

This technology also opens the way to fascinating glass structures using much less material – if the availability using sizes and thicknesses could be improved. In this way the advantages of glass in strength, life span, scratch-resistance and cleaning ease could be used for giving an unobstructed view of the beautiful underwater world of the aquarium.

Waterwall Concept for Eco-House

Diest, Belgium, 1998

"Water, Weed, Glass"

The eco-house was a competition in Belgium held by the Flemish authorities in 1998 to improve the knowledge of sustainable building and to stimulate the use of this type of technology. Architects were invited to design a house featuring a new attitude to ecological building. Together with the architect Bart Biermans and his firm META we ventilated some wild ideas that yet seemed realistic.

The waterwall consists of double glass screens set into a curved 3D steel frame made of hollow sections. The layers and dimensions of the glass

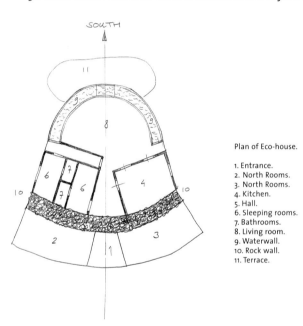

Plan of Eco-house.

1. Entrance.
2. North Rooms.
3. North Rooms.
4. Kitchen.
5. Hall.
6. Sleeping rooms.
7. Bathrooms.
8. Living room.
9. Waterwall.
10. Rock wall.
11. Terrace.

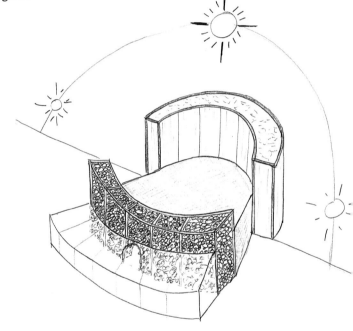

Isometric view of eco-house.
In front the water wall, in the back the rock wall.

would vary depending on the size of the panels, from 3 x 6 mm (small) to 4 x 19 mm (large) toughened glass. As in the case of the Artis aquariums, the water pressure "pushes" the joints watertight. Filled with water in early spring, the waterwall softens the sunlight, an effect enhanced by water thyme, a fast-growing waterweed. In summer the water thyme grows explosively so that a natural, green wall filters the sunlight. The mass of water also keeps out the heat of the sun. After emptying the wall at the end of autumn, the large quantity of water thyme can serve as fodder.

Although the architects discontinued the cooperation on this project and nothing was presented, the design became a source of inspiration for a water roof (see page 134).

Retaining Wall Concept and Transparant Dyke Concept

1997

"Natural Wonderwall"

Retaining walls are mostly made of steel sheet piling for professional building pits and stapled blocks of natural stones or concrete in gardens. Therefore, usually, the actual retained ground is made invisible. What a big loss! Anyone who ever had the pleasure of seeing a worm slowly digging (or better eating) its way through the earth or watching the busy world of an anthill in an earth-filled glass aquarium will agree that this is fun. The beautiful colours of the earth and the natural stratification of the ground are certainly worth being experienced. Now glass is a non-corrosive material and also waterproof.

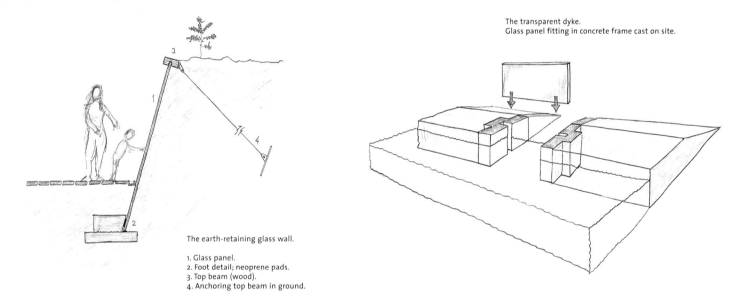

The earth-retaining glass wall.

1. Glass panel.
2. Foot detail; neoprene pads.
3. Top beam (wood).
4. Anchoring top beam in ground.

The transparent dyke.
Glass panel fitting in concrete frame cast on site.

Combining it with the Artis Aquarium detail for the vertical joints leads towards an earth-retaining glass wall. Driving in sheets of thick glass panels is technically feasible as well. So nothing can stop the creation of a true glass retaining wall, which comes complete, as sketched, with a top beam and anchoring.

Concerning the vast field between landscape architecture and art, there once was a proposal by an artist to cut open a dyke and install a glass panel to show the rise and fall of the tide. Such an idea is blasphemy in the Netherlands – no one dares to touch the dykes except to raise them by another meter – so it was sneered at and pushed aside. It is a shame we never met. I think it can be done, as the following sketch should demonstrate.

Flexible Dyke-Top Concept

Deventer, The Netherlands, 1999

"Moving as a Load-Bearing Strategy"

In many a Dutch town a river flows through the town centre.
In Deventer, the river Ijssel brought wealth to the town in medieval days, as
the historic centre still shows. But rivers have the unpleasant tendency to rise
to surprisingly high levels, thus flooding the cellars and ground floors of the
houses on their banks.

In the past a small dyke had been erected in Deventer; raising
this dyke further, a common procedure in the Netherlands, would mean that
the view of the river would be blocked.

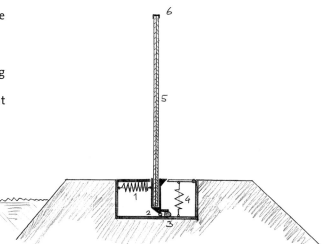

Structure of the flexible dyke-top.

1. Steel spring to stabilize glass wall.
2. Hinge at bottom glass wall.
3. Water proofing by neoprene bar.
(When the glass wall starts to bend,
the bar gets more compressed/
waterproof.)
4. Steel spring to return top-lid to
normal position after high water.
5. Water-retaining glass wall.
6. Stainless steel top protection.

The dyke-top concept responds to both interests. Wouldn't it be nicer
to watch the water rise (through the glass) and, if the water rose to a level reached
only once every 250 years, have it flood over the glass-top in a controlled movement?

The structure responding to these reflections was inspired by the
typically Dutch concept that men have to bend their heads in obedience to the
inevitable will of God. A glass panel is mounted on a hinge fastened onto a concrete foundation. At about 0.5 m above the hinge there is a spring attached to
the glass panel. The rising water pushes against the glass, and the spring and
the glass will gradually deform, until finally the water starts to run over the top
of the panel.

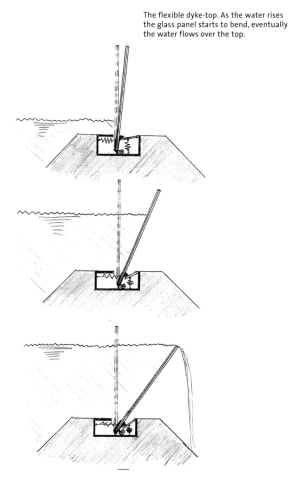

The flexible dyke-top. As the water rises
the glass panel starts to bend, eventually
the water flows over the top.

Glass Windshields

Nijmegen, The Netherlands, 1998

"Clear View, No Wind"

Additional support for the beam running over the glass windshields was reduced to a minimum thanks to the lateral stability provided by the glass panels.

View of the big beam running over the glass windshields. In the centre the edge glass panel of a windshield, supported only at two edges.

Part of an ambitious plan to modernize the railway station area of the city of Nijmegen (see pages 40–41 and 52–53) was a new bus station. Like most Dutch bus stations it was to consist of 10 to 15 parallel stops and a big beam above showing destinations and departure times. The architects wanted glass walls separating the different stops, thus providing shelter from the wind. The glass walls, 3 m high, were to support the information beam.

This is technically possible but would require glass of about the same thickness as for the Artis aquarium tanks (see page 112). As costs proved

A simple wall of 3-m-high, 1.5-m-wide vertical glass panels of 2 x 10 mm toughened glass. In order to reduce the proportion of thickness to size, a steel support is installed, which reaches up to half of the total height. Another cost-saving measure is that there are no boltholes in the glass. Instead, the bolt axis crosses the vertical joint between two panels.

Isometric view of glass windshield at Nijmegen.

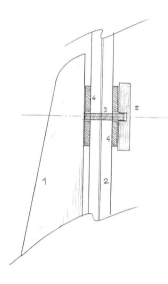

Connecting detail of windshield.

1. Steel support.
2. Glass panel.
3. Bolt welded to 1.
4. Circular neoprene pad.
5. Stainless steel cover plate with internal thread.

to be a fatal bottleneck for this concept, the question arose once more of how to combine glass with other materials and techniques which would interfere as little as possible with its visual elegance. The suggestion was to use tapered steel fins, reaching halfway up the panel and by their support allowing to reduce the glass dimensions. The big beam was to be partly supported by steel tubes and strips. In order to reduce the dimensions of the steel structure to a minimum, i.e. to a degree that would in itself no longer be able to carry the beam, we used the lateral support provided by the glass panels.

Basically, this is a nice and effective solution, but when one of the support glass panels had to be replaced because it had been damaged by hooligans, it was necessary to develop an extensive procedure for doing this safely.

A look through the sequence of glass windshields, giving a greening effect.

Simple connection detail of a 3-m-high panel.

GLASS ROOFS

"How often have I heard disbelief when I explained the La Vilette glass solution
to a control engineer? 'That would not be possible here!' is the response, before
the engineer has examined the argument and with the visible evidence of a
complete structure to go and see.
As if gravity, or the thickness of the window, could somehow change as you
cross the border from France into Germany, or Switzerland or wherever."

Peter Rice
("An engineer imagines", Zurich 1993)

Dutch Pavilion for the EXPO 1998
Lisbon, Portugal, 1998

Glass Dome, Tower of London
London, Great Britain, 1999

Corrugated Glass Roof for Galleria
Rotterdam, The Netherlands, 1993 – 1995

Glass Cone
Zwolle, The Netherlands, 1995 – 1996

Awning, Shopping Mall
Hengelo, The Netherlands, 1997 – 1999
with a note on a glass balustrade for the Royal Theatre
The Hague, 1997 – 1998

Water Roof, City Theatre
Almere, The Netherlands, 1998

Glass Roof Concept for University Library
Utrecht, The Netherlands, 1997 – 2003

Mobile Glass Pavilion
Rotterdam, The Netherlands, 2000 – 2001

Structural Skylight Concept for the University of Venice
Venice, Italy, 1998

Looking up in the atrium of the Leiden City Hall.
Very slender and elegant steel trusses carry
a glass roof with integrated smoke hatches.

The roof is the least prominent part of a building. But due to the increasing density in our cities the roof becomes, as it is sometimes called, the fifth façade. More and more people look down from their high-rise apartment towers and offices on the roofs of the lower buildings. So aesthetical attention for the roof is required. This leads mainly to all kinds of vegetation on the roof varying from grass to complete trees.

The main task of the roof is to protect us from the climate, the cold and the wind, but most of all the rain. And although the famous Dutch architect Gerrit Rietveld is supposed to have said that his buildings are architecture so therefore they have to leak, we cannot accept this.

Careful detailing of the roof and all its connections is essential. Constant care has to be given to the fact that water can stream down the roof easily, without any obstructions on its way. So each roof has to have an angle, a slope to guarantee this. The minimal slope is 5 degrees; at this angle water drops start to move due to the pull of gravity. Less than 5 degrees is asking for trouble, and substantially more attention has to be given to the details, especially regarding the life cycle of the various materials.

Glass roofs, for instance of conservatories, have always been a popular item since the generous inflow of light creates agreeable circumstances. As roofs can be seen as horizontal façades, we find the same type of problems as at façades. For instance, if we are able to increase the thermal insulation of the roof by using double (or insulating) glass, with the favourable aspect of reducing heating energy consumption in winter, the warming up due to the greenhouse effect in summer is considerable. Measures to keep the sun out can be taken. Best is to put a sunscreen outside, on top of the roof, because here the warmth due to the heating-up of the sunscreens will not lead to a rise of the temperature inside. An old method used in garden greenhouses was to put chalk paint on top of the glass in springtime. The white of the chalk reflects the sun but allows the light, at a reduced level, to reach the inside of the building. An advantage of this solution is that in autumn the chalk can be easily washed away, so in winter the welcome warmth of the sun can reach the inside of the building.

In the Budapest project (see pages 24–27), which has a big glass roof (at an angle of 5 degrees), the problem of the summer sun was solved by putting steel grills on top of the glass roof. One of the vertical strips of the steel grid was in line with the average position of the sun in that location, 47 degrees; the other was perpendicular. If the grill was put in the correct position in one direction, the sun was blocked almost completely but, when looking from below through the mesh, the clouds could still be seen. Like the chalk paint, the grills are put on the roof in spring and taken away in autumn. Thus best sun conditions, with regard to the inner climate of the building, can be achieved for every season.

To make a safe roof we have to use laminated glass. As the roof is situated over our heads, we have to avoid scores of tiny sharp glass fragments falling down if a glass panel chances to break. Some people say that toughened glass could be used as well since only a shower of very small parts would come down when this type of glass breaks. Experience has proved, however, that even from toughened glass larger parts can come down resulting in the same threatening situation as with normal float glass.

In this chapter a few special roofs will be dealt with. One project is indeed completely contrary to the good advice we have given here: a horizontal glass roof with water permanently on top of it. It shows that if we keep paying good attention to all different demands we can solve even this challenge with the means of the technologies we have nowadays!

The 90 x 200 m roof covering the Burgers Bush in Arnhem. The roof is formed by inflated plastic cushions providing an almost undisturbed inflow of daylight, minimized weight and optimal heat insulation.

The principle of balancing, the effect of an inclined pylon.

Dutch Pavilion for the EXPO 1998

Lisbon, Portugal, 1998

"To Be or Not to Be Dutch"

The 1998 World Exposition was given the motto: The Oceans – a
Heritage for the Future. On a beautifully situated stretch of land on the banks
of the river Tagus large so-called shadow halls were built to house the presentations of the participants. The theme of the Dutch pavilion was the North Sea,
the Dutch *mare nostrum*, and its architect, Frank Wintermans, had the wonderful
idea of letting the people enter the Dutch pavilion by climbing up a dyke under
an undulating roof of grey and green glass that represented the sea. As this setting was sheltered in the large shadow hall, it proved to be a daring combination

Complete plan of the glass panels forming the dyke roof.
Each element is different.

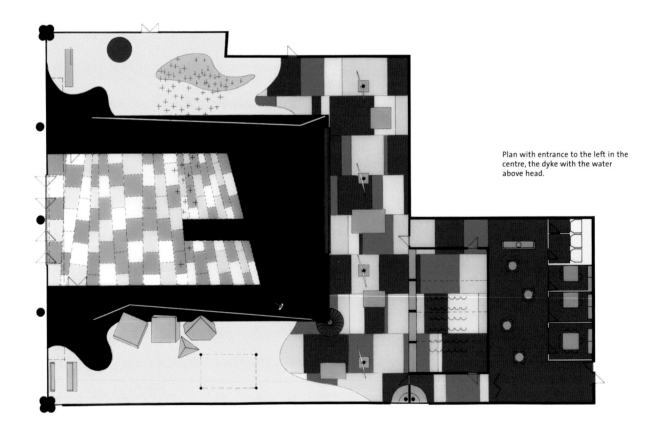

Plan with entrance to the left in the
centre, the dyke with the water
above head.

Side view of the glass wave over the entrance dyke. In front, concrete blocks from a real dyke in Zeeland, Netherlands, with real crustaceans and seaweed grown on it.

The inclined steel columns have diameters varying from 76 mm to up to 219 mm, depending on their respective lengths and loads. The columns support steel beams in the shape of an inverted T (140 x 140 mm). The T-profiles support the roof panels composed of laminated glass. Laminated glass was used for safety reasons because the panels are situated above the visitors' heads.

of natural and artificial aspects. Installed above this roof, lights would increase and decrease in intensity, side walls made of mirrored glass would create the illusion of a large space, and there would be screams of seagulls and even the smell of salted water. When entering this exhibition it should feel like walking below sea level and breaking through the waves. On top of the dyke (the highest possible Dutch point of view) you would be able to overlook the space of the entire pavilion.

In order to give the pavilion a "North Sea" made of glass, we worked in close collaboration with the architect to develop a forest of oblique steel-tube columns, varying in height from 3 to 6 m. By clamping the columns in the steel structure of the dyke it was possible to create a very stable roof, despite the somewhat alarming view of the undulating glass skin on top of

Top view of the glass wave.
In the centre the small entrance
to the Dutch pavilion.

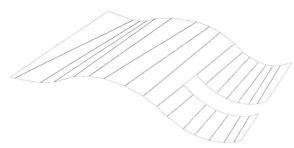

Each of the 106 panels has a different shape, but each is made from 2 x 10 mm plates of glass, which are both annealed. The top plate is so-called "cathedral glass" with a very rough surface, the bottom plate is coloured glass, varying from green to blue. The colouring is done to imitate the experience of being under water.

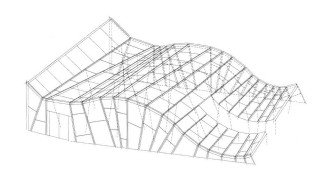

Isometric representation of the steel structure of the glass wave and the glass panels to be placed on top of it.

drunkenly oblique columns. On top of each column a steel shoe was placed carrying a glass beam which, due to the obliqueness of the columns, is also tilted, thereby providing favourable support for the glass panels forming the "surface" of the sea. But tilting a slender glass beam introduced a rotating moment, something very unfavourable for a single slender rectangular beam. To eliminate this twisting moment an (extra) horizontal beam was placed on top of the (more or less) vertical beam. This provided a better support for the glass panels forming the roof surface. The architect selected for the surface of the sea an old type of so-called figured glass, a glass type with a rough, uneven surface, and combined it with a second layer of green or blue float glass.

When the roof was ready to be tendered out in combination with the steel structure for the dyke, a problem arose: one of the sponsors, a glass

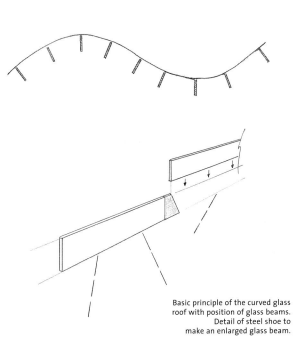

Basic principle of the curved glass roof with position of glass beams. Detail of steel shoe to make an enlarged glass beam.

firm, considered making a contribution, not in money but in material. It took long painful meetings to convince their technical advisors of the strength of this unique structural design. However, in the meantime the financial feasibility of the complete project was under severe pressure. The argument was put forward to the client that a steel beam would not cost anything at all and that in this wild undersea forest the effect of glass beams would be minimal. So the one element that would have dramatically emphasized the undersea effect slipped out through the backdoor, offered on the altars of modern financing. The overall illusion of walking on the bottom of the sea was very nice, also due to the artificial lighting from above, but those who knew the original design kept seeing very disturbing thick lines of steel.

The space under the glass wave through which the visitors walk up the dyke to get into the Dutch Pavilion. Varying top lights shining through the different colours of the glass wave, the sound of waves and the forest of oblique columns gave the impression of walking under water.

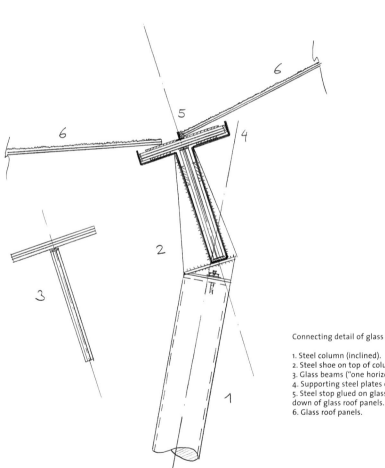

Connecting detail of glass beam to curved glass roof.

1. Steel column (inclined).
2. Steel shoe on top of column.
3. Glass beams ("one horizontal, one vertical").
4. Supporting steel plates of shoe.
5. Steel stop glued on glass beam to stop the sliding down of glass roof panels.
6. Glass roof panels.

Two typical glass panels with different colours and different glass textures chosen to represent the image of a wavy water surface.

Glass Dome, Tower of London

London, Great Britain, 1999

"A Crown for the People"

Intensive use weighs down heavily on buildings, especially if they are the aim of mass tourism. The immediate surroundings of the Tower of London, one of the most important tourist attractions in the city, suffered from premature wear. This problem, together with the long waits caused by the fact that the site was not designed for such large numbers of visitors, induced the authorities to ask a number of renowned architects to come up with ideas for restructuring the Tower complex and its immediate surroundings and adjusting them to modern-age demands. Mecanoo was among the invited architectural

The foldable sphere is resting on a glass table in the ABT Office in Arnhem. The glass table-top is a 2 x 10 mm float glass panel resting on four wooden table legs, tree trunks inspired by the Hanover project. The connection of the tree trunk to the glass panel is made by a stainless steel interface.

Plato's five regular solids and their metaphysical symbol.

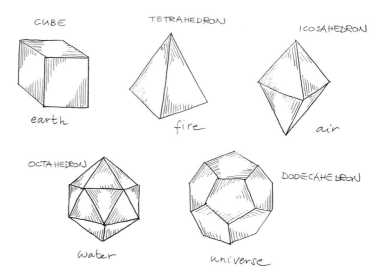

firms, and Francine Houben, responsible for the project, worked out a number of proposals, the central element being a large glass dome. The task of the structural engineer ABT was to convince the jury that this dome could actually be built.

The architectural concept called for a ramp along the Tower complex, which leads the visitors down or rather into the hill housing the ticket office and other facilities. Above their heads the glass dome, letting in light and lending generous space to this underground hall, was projected. Via a ramp, spiralling up, the visitors will leave the dome and enter a majestic boulevard leading to the entrance of the Tower complex, a boulevard with a perfect view on the Thames and the Tower Bridge.

Since the dome was to have a diameter of 15 m, the architects had anticipated that a full-glass structure would be utopian. They suggested a sup-

Icosa-dodecahedron as a bar system.

Icosa-dodecahedron, built up of 20 triangles and 12 pentagons.

The icosa-dodecahedron clad with glass panels, the pentagons have "broken" edges.

port system of gold ribs. The glass panels supported by these ribs were meant to look like ice floes, in other words to sparkle mysteriously at the edges, thereby making the entire structure a giant crown of golden beams and diamonds: a Crown for the People. Its proportions were even modelled after a real crown, including the dent on top.

But how to work out a structure like this? Among the many references mentioned was the glass igloo by artist Mario Merz, but this work of art had some steel joints, which were not only ugly but also could not be blown up to the required scale. Eventually, the idea was to adopt a mathematical approach. A ball can be approached with a polyhedron, or to use its mathematical name, an icosa-dodecahedron. This figure has a total number of 20 triangles and twelve pentagons. For Plato this volume represented "the universe".

The external skeleton of the dome is a set of 2 x 2 ribs made of small metal plates (150 x 150 x 50 mm) glued/welded together to form an elevated arch. The points at which the glass panels are attached are defined according to a mathematical spatial structure, an icosa-dodecahedron. The icosa-dodecahedron is formed by a steel-bar structure, which hangs from the ribs.

Model of the Crown for the People, composed of glass panels with broken edges forming the outside skin and a structural frame of various metals.

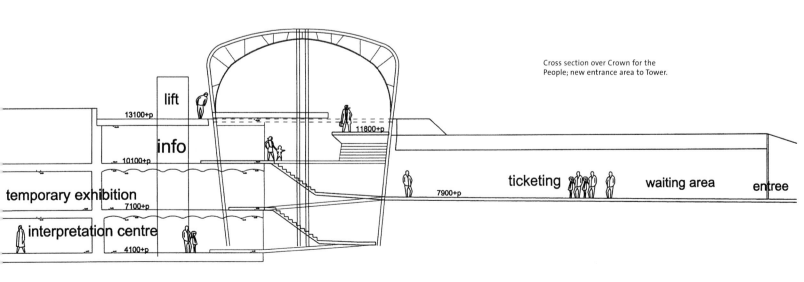

Cross section over Crown for the People; new entrance area to Tower.

lift
13100+p

info
10100+p

temporary exhibition
7100+p

interpretation centre
4100+p

11800+p

7900+p

ticketing   waiting area   entree

From the nice foldable version of this three-dimensional figure, made by the American firm of Hoberman (see picture), we learnt that this structure's pentagons are bigger than the triangles, so we could make the glittering, extending edges to the pentagons while still being able to glue together a regular polyhedron in a ball shape – or, in case the glue was not strong enough, use steel joints to hold the ball together. The supporting ribs surrounding the glass structure were, however, not made of gold, because this would have been far too expensive and also because it would make the crown a welcome target for thieves. Gold also has a low modulus of elasticity and therefore causes a large deformation. Instead a multi-material version – iron, lead, copper, tin, bronze, zirconium, titanium, aluminium, vanadium, uranium, platinum, silver, gold, antimony, to mention just a few – was used for welding/melting a 50-mm-thick

Detail connection of the glass panels
of the icosa-dodecahedron.

1. Steel hollow section of icosa-dodecahedron.
2. Glass panel; triangle.
3. Glass panel; pentagon with "broken" edges.
4. Steel bolt-clamp.
5. Glued connection.

All glass panels have irregular edges, "broken" as the architect calls it, and are made of 2 x 12 mm toughened glass. With regard to the rather large forces and the outside climate all connections of the glass panels to the steel frame of the icosa-dodecahedron are bolted through.

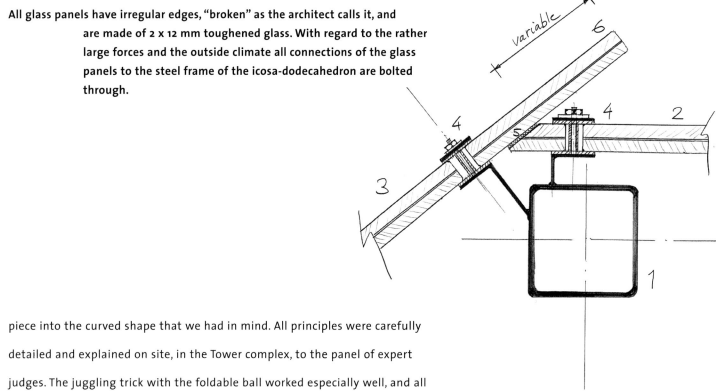

piece into the curved shape that we had in mind. All principles were carefully detailed and explained on site, in the Tower complex, to the panel of expert judges. The juggling trick with the foldable ball worked especially well, and all critical questions as to the technological issues were answered satisfactorily – or so we thought. The jury, however, opted for another project, making this beautiful image, a Crown for all People, part of the heritage of the England that was never built.

Corrugated Glass Roof for Galleria

Rotterdam, The Netherlands, 1993 – 1995

"Curiosity Kills the Cat"

Often the ways of "Big Money" are incomprehensible, but sometimes you are able to discover their pattern. For the prestigious Kop van Zuid – a city development plan in Rotterdam – the City of Rotterdam and property developers agreed that developers would build large office buildings, while the government intended to rent most of them. In return, the developers undertook to build a glass roof in between the office blocks to provide a covered walkway leading from the underground to the adjacent buildings. This deal meant of course that the profit on the whole project would be reduced by the building

Birds-eye view of the proposed structure of the Galleria. An undulating blanket of glass rests on top of asymmetric steel trees.

costs of the roof. The roof was named "Galleria" in order to bring an Italian atmosphere to the sometimes grey and rainy Rotterdam.

Architects Moshé Zwarts and Rein Jansma were commissioned with the roof design and came up with an inspiring structure in which a corrugated glass-skin hovered over the tops of steel trees (meant to be as realistic as possible). For the structural translation (and building cost estimate) of this catching design we first worked out, together with the structurally very proficient architects, the steel trees, starting from the principle of the trunk as a bundle of nine tubes, continuing with three big branches of three tubes each, then nine branches of one tube each and reaching finally 27 twigs made of small tubes, each group of three of them taking the shape of an upsidedown pyramid.

Views from various angles at the main connection of steel tree to glass blanket.

Connection of roof glass panels to steel trees. The wheel can rotate in X, Y and Z direction, and the vertical steel axis can be adjusted to the required length by screwing the vertical axis in or out of the wheel. The little disc on top of the vertical axis can also rotate freely. A drop of glue (silicone) on this disc connects the glass panel of the roof to the structure of the steel trees.

It was on and between these pyramids that the glass panels were placed. For the connection of the glass panels to the final steel parts of the pyramids a very sophisticated detail was developed. Shaped like a wheel, it not only gives the proper support to the glass panels but it also solves in one single detail the problems of all possible spatial deviations and production variations.

By rotating and tilting the wheel the most effective position for the wheel could be fixed. On various points threaded bars could be turned in and out of the wheel to correct the height. On top of each threaded bar a hinged plate was connected on which the glass panels on the roof were glued. Careful computer calculations of all the different types of trees in varying shapes were made in order to check the dimensions and especially the deformation of the trees. To be able to create a corrugated surface we decided to use triangular panels. Each of the three dimensionally curved surfaces can be described best by flat triangular plates that tilt at each joint if one wishes (to reduce costs) to use only flat plates. Horizontal stability was provided for naturally by the big glass plane of the roof itself, clamped in between buildings. But because broken panels could cause local instability – in spite of the fact that they were laminated – the tops of the trees were connected by a horizontal ladder-frame, a sort of spine, firmly attached to the adjacent buildings.

The design team congratulated itself on this ingenious solution and the beautiful design, and although the required building costs were rather high, some representatives of our client was also enthusiastic, others considered the costs to be too high. We were asked to get in touch with capable firms, certainly with the assumption that once production firms bring in their visions and

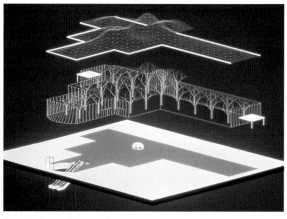

Computer image of the complete steel structure, with the glass panels on top of it.

Steel trees in variable shapes support on the top end of their highest branches / twigs a uniform detail shaped like a wheel. To this wheel (tolerance free) points were connected on which the glass panels of the roof were glued (silicone base). Each plate consists of 2 x 10 mm toughened glass. The joints are simply silicone, glued on site.

Computer image of the Galleria interior. The steel trees are composed according to the bundled-steel-tube concept.

ideas, costs could be reduced. These contacts proved very confusing and contradictory in their results, but we managed to produce documents, and the Galleria roof was put to tender. We had estimated the costs to be about 2 mill. Euro, but all offers were in the 6 mill. Euro region. The client was furious. We were angry and flabbergasted, too, so we decided that since there was little chance to get a good price in the Netherlands we should ask for prices abroad. Eventually, we got an offer from a German firm that was close to our estimate. But it was too late, we were no longer received with open arms and even had to consult lawyers in order to defend our interests vis-à-vis the client. Another more flexible architect got a new commission and a glass roof was realized indeed, but the cultural impact seems very small: it looks like a greenhouse to me. My heart aches whenever I come by this place, still called so cheerfully Galleria.

Glass Cone

Zwolle, The Netherlands, 1995 – 1996

"Gone in Daytime, Present at Night"

For the conversion of an old building into a modern lawyers' office in the city of Zwolle the architect wanted to have a cone-shaped skylight. This had to be as "glassy" as possible, so we were asked to make a structural design. Of course, as always the budget was tight and to make an insulated glass cone proved to be too expensive.

The rounded shape of the cone, which is technically feasible, was also expensive. So to reduce costs we changed the cone into a multi-facetted pyramid, each panel consisting of one layer of glass. This is not at all in accordance

The cone-shaped glass skylight.

This cone (height 2.50 m) is divided into eight facets. The glass panels are made from 10-mm-thick toughened glass. 500 mm under the top the panels are connected by means of steel clamps. On top of the cone a stainless steel cone provides a suitable ending.

with energy-efficiency standards, but if you do it quietly no one will take notice (I hope). This made the basic design a very simple one. Nice details are the foot holding the footprint of the pyramid and a simple bolted connection at the top. The real top was the only luxury we permitted ourselves: a stainless steel top cone, thus no maintenance and a 100 percent waterproof construction.

Two nice, not really intentional effects presented themselves after the realization. The first was the fact that at daytime the pyramid is "not there", just a glass cover for a hole in the roof allowing sunshine to fill the room, a library, actually. But at night, lit from below, the pyramid jumps up from the roof changing the contours of the building. The second effect is even more surprising. In winter, when it freezes hard, the condensation on the inside freezes into beautiful patterns, the so-called ice-flowers.

For the condensed water we had made small internal gutters which would hold the water till it evaporated during the day.

Especially in the house the ice-flower effect is enchanting. In the old days of non-insulation this effect, teaching children about fractal mathematics, could be seen on every windowpane. Energy-saving standards have expelled this natural phenomenon from our daily lives and have robbed human society of a precious gem.

Nightscape. The cone suddenly emerges from the plain of the roof when lighted from below. It begins a conversation with its big brother in the background, the bell tower of the Zwolle Church.

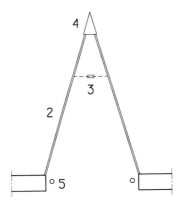

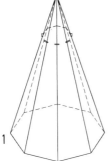

The realised glass cone.

1. Isometric representation.
2. Glass panels.
3. Stainless steel top.
4. Central heating tube preventing the fall of cold air.

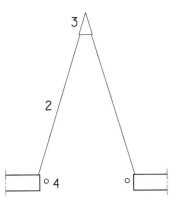

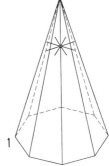

An unrealized version of the glass cone with insulated glass.

1. Isometric representation.
2. Glass panels.
3. Steel connection detail using tension to hold the glass panels together.
4. Stainless steel top.
5. Central heating tube preventing the fall of cold air.

Connection detail of the realized version.

1. Stainless steel plates.
2. Glass panels.
3. Neoprene interlayer.
4. Stainless steel bolt M16.

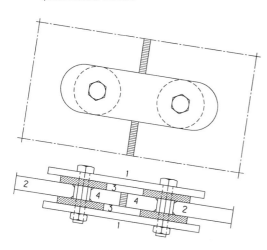

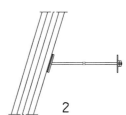

Details of the unrealized version.

1. Connection of insulated glass panel.
2. Glued connection of steel detail.
3. Gutter detail.

Awning, Shopping Mall

Hengelo, The Netherlands, 1997 – 1999

"Horizontal Capacity, the Proof of the Pudding is in the Eating."

The Hengelo awning is a small modest structure, with the beauty hidden, I am afraid, in the details. To provide a dry walk for window shoppers a 2 m cantilevering glass panel was installed above the windows of the shops. On top of the shops, apartments were to be built. The challenge in such a task is always to take up the tensile bending stresses at the support. This requires a flexible detailing which allows the bending moment to be taken up inside the connecting detail. It also requires an extra-careful treatment and protection of the glass panel's surface near the support. It is best to use toughened glass

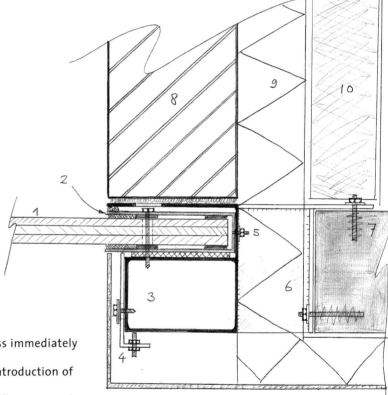

Connecting detail of canopy in Hengelo.

1. Cantilever; glass panel.
2. Steel channel connected with neoprene pads to glass.
3. Supporting hollow section.
4. Vertical correction.
5. Horizontal correction.
6. Connection hollow section to concrete floor.
7. Concrete floor.
8. Brick wall (façade).
9. Insulation.
10. Inner wall.

since this allows some scratches on the surface without the glass immediately breaking. So a sophisticated detail was developed to solve the introduction of the clamping moment. Its principle is to let concentrated forces flow into and from the glass "elastically".

The incorporation into the wall was perfectly detailed too: nothing out of the ordinary, just a nice structural engineering job, which normally nobody would notice. But then suspicious questions were asked. What if somebody dropped a flowerpot – by accident – from the seventh floor onto the awning? Or how can we clean the glass surface – for only a fool would be willing to walk over this dangerously cantilevering glass panel? No series of careful calculations, approved by authorities, was able to dispel such doubts. So we opted for a test on site. Since we also wanted to know when the (steel) glass clamping detail would fail we were given permission to test one panel to failure. The test brought the result that it was impossible to break the panel. It carried 800 kilos for three hours without any sign of cracking.

In this context another test was carried out a year later, this time for a balustrade in the prestigious Royal Theatre of our parliament and government city, The Hague. Here an all-glass balustrade had to prevent people from falling into a deep void. Standards for such a case demand a line-load of 300 kg/m² at a height of 1.20 m above the floor – quite understandably, for a crowd in panic can certainly cause such a load. People, however, were concerned about the long-term behaviour of this structure. Convinced by the swaying of the sandbags, they did not doubt that a short duration load could be taken, but what if a crowd kept pushing for a longer time? The long-term behaviour of

Central stair of the Royal Theatre in The Hague (Architect: Charles van den Hoven).
The glass balustrades have to resist a queuing mass.

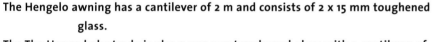

The Hengelo awning has a cantilever of 2 m and consists of 2 x 15 mm toughened glass.
The The Hague balustrade is also 2 x 15 mm toughened glass with a cantilever of 1.20 m.

The total test load on the glass panel, 800 kg of sand sacks.

Steel detail clamping the cantilevering glass plate of the awning.

laminated glass is still somewhat mysterious, so we opted for a test here as well. It was agreed that should the panels hold a line-load of 1.5 x 300 = 450 kilos for three hours the structure would be considered safe. They did. And one panel was even left to carry this massive load for a whole weekend. To our surprise we discovered that the deformation of the laminated panel under this big static load came to a standstill after about 2 hours and increased only little during the weekend. The resulting deformation of the laminated panel was about 25 % less then the deformation of 3 loose panels. Up to this moment we had assumed that this type of load would continue to show increased deformation up to the effect exerted on loose stacked panels. It seems that a kind of equilibrium of shear transfer in the pvb-foil can be achieved under big static loads.

Water Roof, City Theatre

Almere, The Netherlands, 1998

"Walking under Water"

Working with architect Wiel Arets for the proposal he submitted in the international competition for the Almere Theatre, I was impressed by the abstraction, clearness and sense of space in his design. A special accent was given to the entrance hall and the theatre foyers, situated on the lakeside and partly in the lake.

A few months earlier I had walked in the Educatorium in a corridor under a skylight covered with a small layer of water. The position of the sun, together with the wind, created a fairytale-like light, shining through the water

Supported by a primary steel structure, glass beams make the secondary span. The selected span of 5 m and the centre-to-centre distance of 2 m required beams with a depth of 500 mm and a thickness of 9 x 15 mm annealed glass or alternatively 5 x 15 mm toughened glass.

Placed on top of the glass beams, glass panels of 4 x 10 mm toughened glass form the bottom of a "transparent pond on the roof", which is 500 mm deep. For the critical joint between the glass panels, which has to be waterproof, we used the "Artis" aquarium detail (see pages 112 – 113).

with its small waves and its green colour, caused by the algae. I could not get this stunning image out of my head, and working out the construction of the hall I remembered that Almere is in the polder, "under water". The ensuing suggestion was to cover the theatre roof with a layer of water (only in summer, of course). The earlier proposal for the eco-house waterwall involved a water thyme sunscreen (see page 114). What could be more pleasant than walking under water on a sunny summer's day enjoying the light, filtered mysteriously by small waves and water thyme?

Wiel Arets thought it was a splendid idea, but in the final design stages he feared that because of the risk of leakage the jury might decide against his plan. And out went the water roof! It made no difference, as the jury decided in favour of the design by the Japanese architectural firm SANAA.

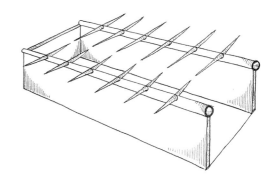

Supporting structure of hall with waterroof, Almere City Theatre.

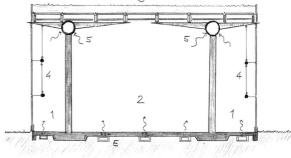

Cross section the hall, Almere City Theatre.

1. Concrete floor with air-supply ducts.
2. Hall/foyer.
3. Water on roof.
4. Massive steel bar-stabilized façade.
5. Steel tube as primary beam which also acts as air-extract duct.

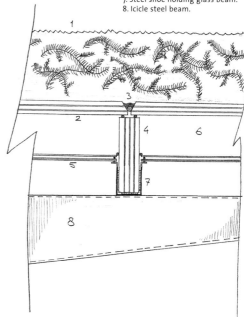

Detail of the waterroof.

1. Water with water thyme.
2. Glass panel (to carry water).
3. Artis aquarium detail (first line of defence).
4. Glass beam.
5. Insulating glass panel (second line of defence).
6. Cavity.
7. Steel shoe holding glass beam.
8. Icicle steel beam.

Glass Roof Concept for University Library

Utrecht, The Netherlands, 1997 – 2003

"Glass and Wood"

Wiel Arets' ambitious design for the new library inspired also the development of a glass roof system that combines internal and external functions of the "fifth façade" (= roof) in a way that only glass can achieve. In his vision the library will be a combination of concrete boxes containing books and voids, surrounded by an intelligent glass façade providing sun-control and individually controllable natural ventilation. The roof concept calls for a combination of waterproofing and rainwater draining on the outside, and the indoor use of the air that is heated by the sun directly under the glass of the roof.

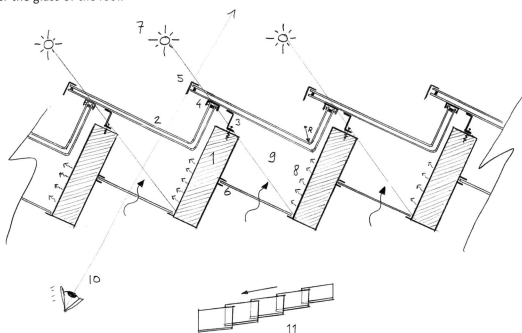

The industrial capability of making 90-degree-bended glass makes it possible to create tile-shaped elements whose bend may be used to function like the bottom of a gutter. Placing the glass elements on the roof in tile position makes waterproofing in a longitudinal direction easy and creates the desired gutter effect. The "tiles" are placed on laminated wooden beams. By closing the underside of the beams with glass panels a transparent solar-heating duct is formed for the indoor-air heated up by the sun. Large laminated wooden beams, placed at 500 mm centre-to-centre, support the glass panels. All glass dimensions are standard size. This library is now under construction, but on the way to realization the glass roof was replaced by a more economical solution.

Glass roof of library in Utrecht.

1. Inclined laminated wooden beam.
2. Curved insulated glass panel (R = 80 mm).
3. Steel support on top of wooden beam.
4. Inverted U-channel as support of glass panel.
5. Steel angle protecting edge of glass panel.
6. Glass panel providing a "tube-channel" for the air to be extracted.
7. The sun is blocked by the wooden beam so it cannot reach the inside of the building.
8. Sun-heated side of wooden beam (painted black).
9. Air-channel to extract sun-heated air.
10. Clear view of sky from within.
11. Principle of the gutter-shape of panels in roof.

Mobile Glass Pavilion

Rotterdam, The Netherlands, 2000 – 2001

"Glass Kit of Parts"

The mobile dome near the Euromast
in the centre of Rotterdam.

The status of European Cultural Capital brought many activities to Rotterdam in 2001. It was Dirk Jan Postel (see the Rotterdam glass bridge, pages 28 – 29) who put forward the idea to develop a detachable glass dome for this occasion, which could be easily erected at different locations and under which, more or less protected against wind and rain, cultural activities might take place in all kinds of unexpected places. The same team as for the bridge set out, without commission or budget, to develop a project that would hopefully kindle enthusiasm in the people on the other side of the table.

The actual dome is part of a curved spatial plane, 2.50 m from centre-to-centre, corresponding to the catenary (a catenary is the shape a chain takes when hanging between two points). For the structure we chose slender, massive steel bars in an architectural cross section, about 100 x 175 mm.

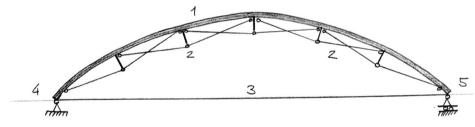

Basic structure of glass dome Rotterdam.

1. Steel arch.
2. Fink-truss-type suspension cables.
3. Steel tie to secure arch.
4. Support; hinge.
5. Support; roll.

A prerequisite was that all elements had to fit, for easy storage and transport, into a few containers. It should also be easy to assemble and dis-assemble the dome, that is with a limited number of four people or so and a light crane, in a maximum of 2 days. With massive steel bars and using the so-called Fink-truss construction an arch is made spanning 30 m and having a height of 6 m in the middle. The mathematical formula for this arch is the inverted chain line. The arch is created by simply bending the steel bar, on the ground, into the shape that has been drawn on the floor and then adding the stiffening trusses. The arch is then lifted and firmly fixed to the supports and a tie connecting its ends. Transversal stability is created by locking a glass panel between each of the steel arches and finally spanning steel cables from side to side. The size of the glass panel is determined by the weight which two men

The mobile dome at a location on the outskirts of Rotterdam.

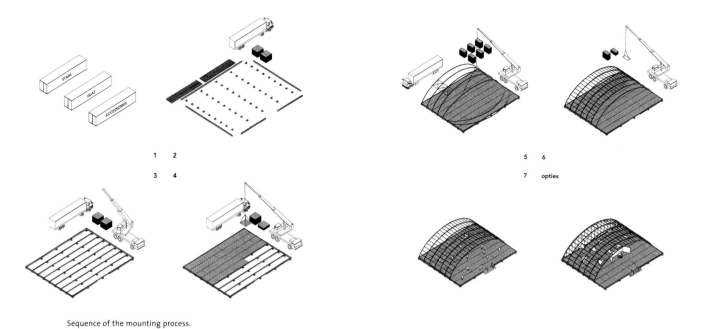

Sequence of the mounting process.

Because of its slenderness this bar is to be stiffened by a so-called Fink-truss system, a type of suspension. The arch thus formed has a span of 30 m. Toughened glass panels (2 x 8 mm) are mounted between the steel bars of the arches. Neoprene wedges clamp the glass between the steel bars so as to provide lateral and transversal stability from the glass plane. For this purpose it is also necessary to span steel cables from one side of the dome to the other.

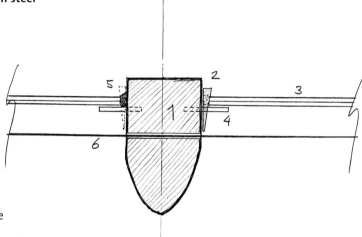

can handle with the help of a sucking-disc device. This turned out to be

2.50 x 1 m. The span makes it possible to reduce the thickness of the panel

to 2 x 8 mm toughened glass.

While a budget was achieved to elaborate details, it became clear

that this beautiful project was never to be built for Rotterdam 2001. But good

ideas never die and that is why it is presented in this book.

Basic detail of glass dome.

1. Steel arch.
2. Hard neoprene wedge.
3. Glass panel.
4. Steel support for 3; neoprene tube around it.
5. Silicone joint for water tightness.
6. Steel cable to tighten the roof together.

Structural Skylight Concept for the University of Venice

Venice, Italy, 1998

"Competition and Death in Venice 1998"

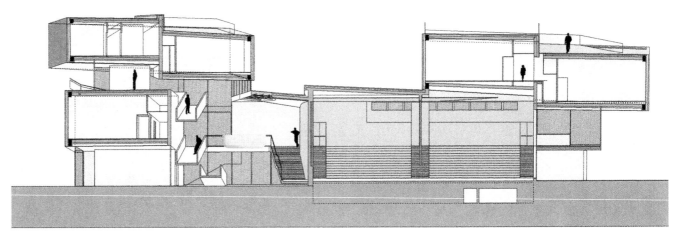

Cross section of the proposed building. The
central space with the stair is the entrance hall,
with the structural skylight in its roof.

How to make a glass-filled hole in a concrete roof.

1. The intact concrete roof is supported at three edges.
2. Based on FEM-calculation, the least-loaded area
of the roof is cut away.
3. A glass panel is inserted, with the steel reinforcement
cast inside it.

1

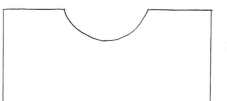

2

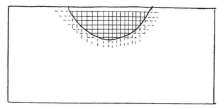

3

Glass and concrete have the same mechanical properties, their resistance is low in tension, but high in compression. Therefore, it would be an obvious thought to replace concrete by glass. For the present example, this idea was based on the strategy of "repairing" a hole cut into a concrete roof.

In a competition for a new building for the Venice University Institute of Architecture, the design of two young architects, Karl Amann from Germany and Giuseppe Mantia from Italy, reached the final selection round. The two had met at the Berlage Institute in Amsterdam, where I came to know them later as a teacher in structural engineering. The beautiful design they made, with a Venetian-style brickwork façade, placed the auditoriums in the centre of a spiral. The adjacent entrance hall had a big skylight for taking in the Italian natural light. It was possible for us to determine the shape of the opening according to engineering requirements, using a finite-element computer calculation in order to define an area where the concrete should be cut away and replaced by glass. In this way it was possible to identify the sections which would deform most while having small bending moments due to the proximity of the supporting walls.

The regular solution would have been to use a glass plate hanging free in the hole and supported by the edges of the hole. Instead, we decided to actually incorporate the glass plate into the concrete roof. This would mean connecting the glass structurally to the concrete. Such a structural connection would imply less deformation and thus the possibility of reducing reinforcement in the concrete part of the roof. And from a philosophical point of view it would mean to abandon the notion of a passive glass plate in a cut-out hole and instead

Computer image of the entrance hall with structural skylight.

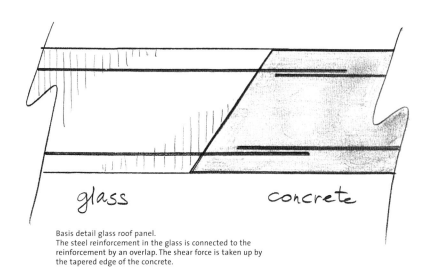

glass   concrete

Basis detail glass roof panel.
The steel reinforcement in the glass is connected to the reinforcement by an overlap. The shear force is taken up by the tapered edge of the concrete.

introduce a structurally active glass plate giving the building more impact. This concept required the use of reinforcement in the glass. The reinforcement can be made from steel or materials like Twaron or Kevlar. Layers of thin steel or Twaron would be inserted into the pvb-foils which glue the individual layers of the glass panel together. The reinforcement of the glass would be connected to the concrete cast on site.

FEM image of the computer calculation for the correct position of the structural skylight.

The jury, however, was not impressed, neither by the intelligent glass plate nor by the beautiful, quiet design fitting the age-old city of Venice like a glove. The design of Karl and Giuseppe became part of the "unbuilt" Venice, but the idea of the structural skylight remains valid.

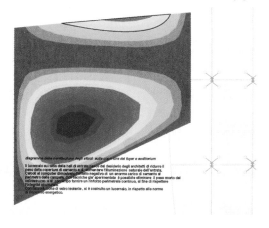

BEYOND GLASS

"Formerly, at the beginning of the Machine Age, the engineer was
often timid and self-effacing. In contrast, the architect was often
pompous, omniscient, trailing clouds of pretension. But things
have changed! The tendency now is for the engineer to be
scornful and aggressive towards the architect enthroned above
him. And so the fight is on! My theory will establish peace and
bring collaboration and efficiency to the aid of the "constructors".
These are the engineer's responsibilities: the respect of the
physical laws and the care for the materials (supply, economical
considerations etc. in relation to safety, relatively speaking).
And these are the architect's: humanism, creative imagination,
love of beauty, and freedom of choice.
The engineer's side must be reflected in that of the architect –
the reflection of the knowledge of physical laws. Similarly, the
architect's understanding of human problems must be reflected
in the side of the engineer."

Le Corbusier
(in: "Science et Vie", August 1960)

Enlighted building: the Educatorium.

Structural letter, the Minnaert
building.

Stacked landscape, not a building,
the Hanover EXPO 2000.

Modern architecture requires modern engineering. This may seem
a platitude, but it is essential for the success of a building designed with the
intention to be something more, something better than commercially oriented
architecture. Better, not only with respect to aesthetic, but also to functional
qualities. To survive the complete trajectory from sketch design to realization the
project must be tough, it has to withstand many enemies trying to eliminate it.
The laws of nature, as Charles Darwin described them, also apply to building
projects: only the fittest survive. Fittest, not only in their qualities (nature), but
also in the way they have grown up (nurture). They need to have good parents
who nourish and guard the project. Only then a special type of design will
survive and become realized.

In this chapter three extraordinary projects are described. The fact
that they were realized indicates that they have special qualities, but also that
they had good and able parents in form of the clients, the architects, the advisors
and last but not least the contractors.

In the Educatorium the main design issue was the circulation of people in this building which was to serve a central function for the University of Utrecht. This circulation is visible in the design; a floor moves slowly up in a ramp-like walkway, starts to become a wall and after sharply bending over becomes the roof. This basic idea was presented by the architect in one of the first design team meetings by plying a sheet of paper. How to convert this wonderfully simple vision into a real building was a down-to-earth problem for which the structural engineer was hired.

The Minnaert building, owing its name to a famous professor from the first half of the 20th century, was meant to be the central building for another part of the University of Utrecht, the Faculties of Science. Here the architect wanted to make a cave, a friendly place secluded from the rest of the world where the visitors of the building were to be tackled in all their senses: sight, sound, taste/smell and touch. The Minnaert building was meant to offer much in terms of sustainable architecture, not in the sense of using traditional materials but by making our intelligence and techniques work for a better, more sustainable way of life. The structural engineer's task was to integrate these various, sometimes conflicting, interests in one structure.

The design of the Dutch pavilion for the World Exhibition EXPO 2000 in Hanover was a most complicated architectural *tour de force*. It was not only a building, it represented an intriguing philosophy as well: the building was conceived as a "stacked landscape". Each level of the building was to have a different structural system and a different structural material. Furthermore, in order to increase the architectural diversity, the architects did not want columns to be placed on top of each other. These were the structural requirements for constructing this "stacked landscape". The closing line, like in almost all projects, was that the project had to be realized in time and on budget.

Technology can create almost anything, it is above all the budget and the building time which put serious limitations to what can (or should we say may) be achieved. Clients and architects never lack ambition, it is the money which determines the rate of difficulty with regard to realizing a project. The first major problem is the way the budget is established. Quality surveyors have a strong tendency of looking at old, more or less similar projects. Then they interpolate the financial result to the planned project (and last but not least keep a little aside to create the required tension in the project). The second major problem is that contractors do not like new, unfamiliar things. To calculate a price for a project just from examining the tender documents is still just an educated guess at the future. Not every singularity in the design has been sorted out, and the building site, the climate, the available labour source and the skill of the employees remain uncertainties.

So new methods or construction techniques are regarded with extra precaution, for they increase the possible difficulties that contractors later translate into greater building costs. So in the tender document procedures the project must be presented as complete as possible to elimate that uncertainties may possibly occur. For the Educatorium project we worked out a comic book-like presentation to illustrate the construction of a corrugated steel plate roof spanning a lecture room in an arabesque-like undulating way. The selected contractor still regarded it as a difficult, hence expensive, way to build this roof. So we had to work out a simpler system based on small steel beams put very close together, giving only an echo of what could have been a roof rolling over your head like the waves of the ocean. Luckily enough, the roof of the other auditorium survived the critical eye of the contractor. Another lesson is that it is always wise to present two challenges: the chance that one survives is remarkably higher. One aspect of Darwin's laws translated into structural design.

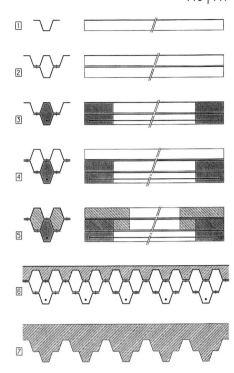

Structural proposal (not realized) for the roof of the C-400 auditorium in the Educatorium.

1. A single panel of corrugated steel is made.
2. Another panel is placed on top of the first one.
3. A steel tie is incorporated in the corrugated steel panel by filling a part with concrete.
4. A third panel of corrugated steel is put on top.
5. Part of the panel is filled with concrete to take up the shear forces at the supports. Now a single element of the roof structure is completed and can be transported from the workshop to the building site.
6. All the elements are placed next to each other and a connecting layer of concrete is poured on top.
7. View of the corrugated underside of the roof.

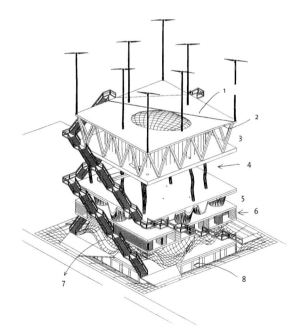

EXPO 2000 Dutch pavilion concept.

1. Water and island.
2. Steel structure.
3. Main exhibtion area.
4. Forest area.
5. Exhibition and services.
6. Agricultural area.
7. Dunes (made with concrete).
8. Cellar (offices etc.).

The Educatorium

The Educatorium is the somewhat posh name for Utrecht University's central building on its Uithof campus on the outskirts of the town. For the Uithof area OMA made a plan which accommodated, with two exceptions that remained in the old city centre, all university faculties.

One of the proposals of the plan was to position a building for general facilities at a central place and to create here the area's "jewel box". The building was to accommodate a restaurant for 1,000 people, two large lecture rooms for 400 and 500 people respectively and examination rooms for a total of 750 people. The building was to be used not only by students and university staff but also for public lectures and conferences, and for the orientation days of secondary school students.

The University Board of Governors commissioned OMA (and the firm's senior architect Rem Koolhaas) with the design of this special building.

Educatorium at dusk. Under the folded concrete blanket is the restaurant for 1,000 people.

The Strategy

The way in which the architects presented their design to me for the first time by means of a piece of paper was characteristic of the project in the sense that it highlighted the essence of the design. The explanation was as follows; the theme of the building is circulation, that is, the continuously changing stream of people in the building. This dynamic aspect resulted in a specific concept. There are two main streams, a horizontal one leading to the restaurant on the ground floor, the other one via a ramp leading up to the lecture and examination rooms on the first floor. Reflections on this movement created the main shape of the building. With a piece of paper the architects showed that by making the paper slant upward, then bending it and making it go back horizontally, a building shape is born naturally. And the fact that the floor of a lecture room is supposed to be rising determined both the position of the lecture rooms and, under the sloping plane, again almost naturally, the creation of a beautiful space for a large restaurant.

The next question, however, was how to build such a "movement in the air"? The architects wanted a visible concrete construction. The shape they devised, therefore, had to be made in concrete, cast on site, which means that a very expensive curved shuttering had to be made. The problem of heat insulation made things even worse. In its desire for minimizing the loss of energy when heating buildings the Dutch government has prohibited the use of so-called cold bridges. This means that a construction must not continue from the inside to the outside without a heat insulation layer interfering at the "crossroads". In terms of the intended shape this meant that the concrete of the floor of the lecture rooms – and the ceiling of the restaurant respectively – was not allowed to jut out, to turn first into outer wall and then into roof. Solving this problem by including a layer of insulation in the shuttering would have made the costly shuttering even more expensive.

We eventually suggested to use shotcrete for the outer wall. In another project, we used this method on a large-scale basis for artificial rocks in a zoo. In this case we suggested the following structure: start with a steel cylinder for the structural transition from floor to wall and roof, add a layer of insulation on top of the shell and use a layer of shotcrete on the outside. Smoothing shotcrete with a spatula when it is not yet dry creates the image of cast concrete. The steel shell to be used was of the simplest and cheapest possible construction: steel round-rolled IPE-sections for ribs covered with a 3-mm-thick steel plate for a skin. Of course, something simple will never stay simple for long: the architects suggested to add a 25-m-wide window to this shell. Fortunately, it was possible to maintain the strength of the shell despite introducing the window opening by applying two diagonal bow shapes. The

Side elevation at night. In the words of the architect this is not a façade but a glazed cross section. At night the building becomes a stage with the visitors/users as actors. The big north truss, hidden in the first floor, creates a 35 m free span in the façade (sit venia verbo) of the restaurant.

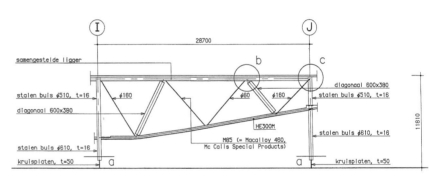

Technical drawing of the north truss. Each element is calculated exactly to state the dimension required for the respective forces.

architects liked the shapes so much that it was decided to leave out the planned false ceiling in order to expose the structural line pattern. Another important issue for them was to be honest in the construction. Therefore, the impression conveyed from the outside that the concrete seems to continue effortlessly is contradicted on the inside by revealing the steel shell.

Although the construction budget was in general sufficient for this type of building, it remained important to use the means in a clever way to create the intended atmosphere and to have available resources for any special architectural demands. The architects suggested to apply a less luxurious approach to the examination rooms in favour of a generous budget for the more public part of the building; the lecture rooms and the restaurant. A fairly industrial steel construction with channel plate floors was opted for. In the overall pattern, the examination room section, conceived as a separate building block on columns, takes the roof-line from the right-hand roof and continous it onto the left-hand one.

The tranversal direction of the building is designed according to requirements of use. The longitudinal direction, as described above, dictates the shape of the building and thus its architecture.

The north truss during construction.

The North Truss

Looking at the Educatorium one is struck by the presence of an anonymous high-rise building from the 1960s looming up behind it. This building to the south of the Educatorium functions like a huge sunblind, an effect very convenient for the architects who wanted the restaurant to be as transparent as possible, especially since to the north the Educatorium is bordered by a park. For these reasons the presence of this 1960s building led to consequences for the positioning of the columns in the Educatorium. At the back of the building, where the kitchen is situated as well, there were few restrictions, but moving to the front, to the park, the number of columns per grid had to decrease and finally be reduced to zero in the façade. The one column left in the last-but-one grid was handled by devising a very special column head, designed first as a half "concrete egg" cut lengthwise and afterwards, for economic reasons, as a steel beam reduced to its elementary shape. The final frame in the façade, however, required more serious thinking. 35 m had to be spanned. Soon we were struck by the fact that the floor above offered an excellent opportunity for adding a storey-high truss, fitting it into the wall between the 500-seat lecture room and the corridor zone. We suggested not to use an anonymous truss with identical or similar diagonals throughout but to demonstrate the specific strength of each diagonal. Thus the compressive forces are absorbed by a thick

The roof of the 500-seat auditorium under construction. On the left the north truss and in the roof the reinforcement coming out of the concrete.

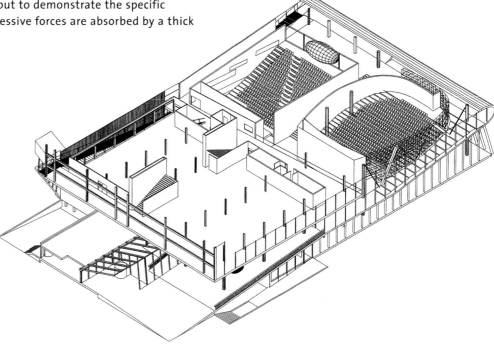

Birds-eye view of the exposed structure. In front one big examination room and in the back the two lecture rooms, the 400-seat one to the left and the 500-seat one to the right. The latter has the reinforcement coming out of the roof.

bar of concrete and the tensile ones by a massive steel bar, its diameter a function of the magnitude of the strength in the bar. This approach created two moments of utter amazement: on the ground floor, where the concrete ceiling of the canteen seems to float at the edge of the façade, and on the first floor, where the frame bars manifest themselves as columns of individually varying sizes that seem to walk cheerfully along the wall of the corridor. A contribution to architecture has been made using the laws of applied mechanics.

Overall Stability

The stability of the entire building was quite a challenge. In some places the service shafts could be used, but these were small and close together. Therefore, the large sloping floor of the outside entrance was mobilized for stability. The horizontal forces of the wind are transported via the floors to this slope that on its turn must transport these forces in its plain to the ground. This floor, however, is outside. For this reason the connection with the inner area is dilated but in such a manner that horizontal forces could be transmitted along the longitudinal axis of the joint. All this was not sufficient either, so in two places a cross or a prop for absorbing tensile or compressive forces was added. Their function having been explained to the architects, they decided not to cover up these elements.

The Roof Floors

The two roof floors of the large lecture rooms are another source of amazement. Here about 20 m had to be spanned. For the 400-seat lecture room, which is on the "dark" side of the building (due to the 1960s building), closed concrete walls were chosen with fixings for acoustic panels and finishings in chipwood print, a subtle echo of the chipwood plate back wall of the lecture room. The roof was to have an undulating, arabesque touch, relating to the roof of the Danstheater in the Hague, an earlier OMA piece of work, as a point of reference. First we experimented with two steel folding plates put on top of each other, a nice and cheap solution but not sufficient for the 20 m span. The next logical step were three steel folding plates, with a layer of concrete added on top for coherence and sound insulation (= mass). This concept also allowed for a steel/concrete cooperation between the compressive side (on top) and the tensile zone (beneath). To this end the tensile zone had to be reinforced with a prestressed steel bar. It was possible to prefabricate the entire pile and only add the concrete upper layer on site. Unfortunately, this construction proved to be inefficient and expensive for the contractor (so he told us) and a cheaper alternative had to be found. The final solution was found in a series of IPE-360 beams (600 mm centre-to-centre), with a single steel folding plate on top, and a concrete layer on top of that. The original system would have created a

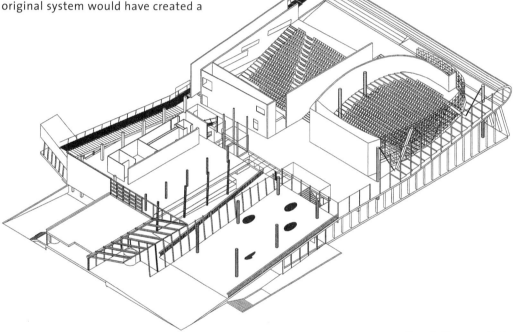

Another birds-eye view of the exposed structure. In front the entrance, sloping up, and in the back the two lecture rooms.

The roof of the 500-seat lecture room, with the exposed reinforcement of the concrete.

beautiful arabesque-like undulation, in a good and efficient construction, and maybe there will come a chance of realizing this idea in another project.

The most surprising construction of the Educatorium is the roof floor of the 500-seat lecture room. It is controversial in the sense that, while the basic idea is very obvious, never before a construction system like this has been used. Again it all starts with the floor-to-wall-to-roof movement, the leitmotiv of the façade – or as we were once reprimanded: the north façade is not a façade but a cross section of the building made visible by closing it with glass. The fold-back movement was made visible in the façade with a Traverine natural stone band. Proportion studies dictated this band to be 400 mm high. As a consequence, in inside-inside situations like the lecture room-restaurant context 400 mm were available for the thickness of the floor. This was more than sufficient. But for the eaves the situation was different: we had to take into account 100 mm insulation and roof covering and another 100 mm for the pitch and the elevation, which meant that for the constructive floor only 200 mm of the 400-mm-thick package was left. And with that we were supposed to span the lecture room of about 20 m!

The task was virtually impossible and led to frequent conferences with the architects. But they were adamant about the 400 mm for the visible façade package. Taking into account the roof load, we needed about 500 – 600 mm of floor depth. All kinds of solutions were discussed, like reducing the size towards the bearings and expanding it in the middle, but these remained strange, unnatural structures involving high building costs. At a brainstorm session once more all kinds of alternatives were discussed like steel sheetpile wall planks, normally used in deep building excavations, steel hanging dishes filled with a layer of concrete or a concrete plate having the required thickness in the middle but reduced to 200 mm at the bearings. A nice solution but not the perfect one. Then somebody asked: "Why do you need a 600 mm height in the middle?"

The answer is simple, of course, for someone familiar with the calculation of structures. Since in the middle of a span there is maximum bend and hence the maximum bending moment, the plate must mobilize the maximum internal moment there; compressive forces at the top and tensile forces at the bottom help to counter the bending. The larger the distance between top (compression) and bottom (tensile forces), the more effectively this is done. And since concrete can absorb hardly any tensile forces, steel reinforcement bars have to be added to bridge the cracks, ensure coherence, absorb the tensile forces and counter the bending.

The structural connection of the 50-mm-thick reinforcement bar to the rest of the reinforcement inside the concrete roof makes an insect-like appearance. Unfortunately, this beautiful, functional detail is hidden inside the concrete forever.

The view from the stage in the 500-seat auditorium. The reinforcement is there but does not disturb the impression of space in the room.

The folded concrete blanket (as seen from the interior) shows what it is in reality: a steel shell structure. The two sets of diagonals allow the creation of a 25-m-wide window on the world.

FEM calculation image of the roof, determining the shape of the part where the reinforcement emerges from the concrete.

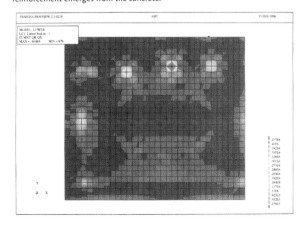

"Hm," was the architects response to our explanation," Why don't we leave out the cracked concrete; it just weighs a lot and it's right in the middle of the span." A clear thought and one worth taking a closer look at.

A floor made of a thin layer of concrete and a steel net of reinforcement bars beneath it behaves differently from a concrete plate of a similar thickness. It is geometrically non-linear, so to speak, and only a powerful finite element computer program which combines all bars and the concrete plate into a computing model is able to calculate this intricate combination with reasonable accuracy. The best model for understanding this phenomenon is the string of a guitar. When you exert sheer perpendicular pressure on the string, it will easily deform at the beginning, but more and more strength will be needed for further deformation.

The first question was: at which point do we make the reinforcement bars come down from the concrete? We first made a simple 200 mm concrete plate model in the proper configuration, loaded it with the expected load and established the failure area in the panel. This area defined the zone where the bars had to come out of the concrete, and its centre was where the lowest point had to be. Unfortunately, this did not coincide with the aesthetic demands of the architect. Some shifting to and fro had to take place to keep all parties satisfied. Calculations were made, dimensions suggested, everything seemed to function well, but the bending, especially the first own-weight bending, was large, about 300 mm. This made us wonder about the next question: how do you construct a floor in which the reinforcement has to come out of the concrete as if by magic?

The most powerful detail of the 500-seat Auditorium. Straightforward, but hard to make, it requires careful and skilful formwork detailing.

The shuttering had to be such that the sagging would be compensated by an upward positioning of the formwork in order to avoid any visible sagging when the support construction was removed. To make implementation easier, a 1220 mm rhythm in the distances of the bars sticking out of the concrete was established, which is half of the shuttering plates' standard of 2440 mm. Thus at each crossing of four plates a round hole could be sawn out for the vertical bar. The primary direction (the shortest side) of the reinforcement coming out of the floor was made in prefabricated steel frames. The primary bar,

A nightscape of the examinations rooms' side of the Educatorium.

round 50 mm, follows the curving of the net, the verticals protrude from the holes in the shuttering and the concrete layer which is 200 mm thick has a bar, round 20 mm, in its centre. The bars, round 16 mm, perpendicular to this direction, the secondary span, had to be welded in after deshuttering.

Thanks to careful consultation with those carrying out the design and especially with the carpenters who made the shuttering everything went according to plan. Worth mentioning is the architect's note in the building specifications stating that the "colour" of the reinforcement bars should be "as rusty as possible"!

We left in the shuttering and the props as long as possible to make sure that the concrete could achieve optimum strength and that maximum shrinkage had taken place. When the exciting moment came and theory was tested in practice, fortunately, there was only a minimum deviation between our calculations and the values measured. To monitor the deformation in time – the creep strain – sagging was measured for one year. The values we found were smaller than predicted. Standing in the lecture room, which is in frequent use, it is pleasing to see that the architect has been able to create the desired 200-mm-thick floor and that the structural engineer got the floor depth he wanted in the middle of the span.

The Minnaert Building

The Minnaert building is the central building of the Science Faculties in the Uithof area of Utrecht University. Professor Minnaert, whose name adorns this building, even in a constructive manner as we shall explain later on, was a much-loved professor from the first half of the 20th century. The building provides the general facilities for the faculties of mathematics, geology, physics and astronomy, all linked with the Minnaert building on the first floor. Lab spaces are on the ground floor. On the first floor a restaurant for 500 people, various information desks, two lecture rooms for 100 people each and finally a large hall of about 20 x 50 m with a height of 8 m are situated. In this hall, the *pièce de résistance* of the building, all circulation streams meet. For the architect Willem Jan Neutelings the list of requirements was so strictly defined that it left him little freedom of design. The only area which had not been defined was the so-called tare space, the additional general-business square meters on top of the net square meters resulting directly from the list of demands. These "grey" square meters became his source of inspiration, they were put together as much as possible and combined into the large hall.

Neutelings also wanted to build in a sustainable manner, but not in the sense of much wood and thick layers of insulation. He wanted to develop clever common-sense suggestions which would save energy without too much technology. He suggested the installation of a gutter system to collect the rain falling onto the building in a large pond. A very large pond indeed: 50 m long, 6 m wide and an average 60 cm deep, holding about 180,000 l of water! Rain water, integrated as so-called grey water in a separate system of ducts in the building, can be used for flushing the toilets and for performing cleaning activities, which is of great importance because about 75 % of the water used in offices every day is grey water! The large quantity of water in the pond can also be used as a buffer for reducing the rapid warming of the building in summer. This effect is even intensified on hot summer days by pumping the water from the pond onto the roof during the night and making it lose a few degrees more by exposing it to the starry sky.

A genuine architectural intervention consisted in channelling the rain water into the pond through five very large funnels opened up in the surface of the roof. The rainwater splashes from the roof into the pond in the hall. This creates a sacral space which addresses all five senses. When it rains you hear the water fall into the pond, you can judge from the level of the water in the pond whether it has rained a lot lately and you can smell the water. As there are hardly any windows in the hall there is a mysterious, somewhat subterranean atmosphere.

Elevation. The skin is made from shotcrete in an earthen terra-cotta colour. The ribbons on the façade act as sundials of some sort, their shadows dictated by the position of the sun.

Big Hall

Conceived as the central circulation space, the hall had to be without columns. An even roof and even walls, without a visible support construction, were to enhance its character as a subterranean space. On the other hand, the hall was intended to be a transition area and therefore only had to be kept frostproof.

The solution for the roof, with a free 20 m span, was found in the catalogue of the prefab concrete industry: standard bridge girders in the shape of fully prestressed concrete, I-girders, 400 mm wide, with a height of 1,250 mm in the middle, optimized by industry to reach the possible limits. These girders could be delivered quickly and at a reasonable price. They were installed on top of the roof, and the concrete roof panels were then fixed to the bottom, thus creating the even, smooth concrete ceiling that the architect had envisaged. All of the visible concrete was made in a yellow pigment, to convey a warm impression. At five points the smooth ceiling is punctured by the funnels. The sidewalls are also made of yellow-coloured prefab concrete. On one side this is an even wall; on the other, the wall is made out of three-dimensional elements. The even walls have a hole/entrance, a very special shape that gives access to small niches for meeting in small groups or for studying. The niches are separate concrete boxes simply hanging on the concrete wall.

The shotcrete façade, its rough texture created by in-blown parts of grit during the process of shotcreting.

The same construction principle was used in the restaurant, but there large non-structural steel/glass columns have been used. At their bottom these columns blow heated air into the room at low speed. The top of the columns lets daylight come in during the day and accommodates artificial lighting for the night. These sources of light are balanced to give always an equal level of light.

Elevation showing the various areas of uses.

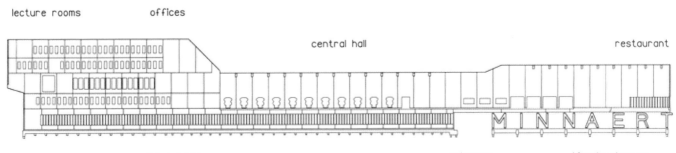

lecture rooms — offices — central hall — restaurant — laboratoria — entrance — bicycle storage — MINNAERT

Letter Columns

One look at the building is enough to clearly recognize its name. The letters M I N N A E R T stand out in the form of columns supporting the building. The name of the building had been selected even before the design had been made. In the architect's first drafts the name was to be installed on the roof using letters of neon light. When exchanging views in a relaxed atmosphere after a long meeting, we were suddenly struck by the fact that the name M I N N A E R T consisted of "stable" letters. They were all perfect pillars and fortunately not an O, an S, a G, or a C was in it, letters which are much more resilient. The decision to use the letters as columns near the bicycle gallery on the ground floor, instead of the customary and rather boring I-shape columns, was quickly made. The columns are steel hollow sections with a diameter of 400 mm. Being part of the main support construction, they were filled with concrete to make them fireproof. Incidentally, the first part of the building rising above the ground happened to be its name!

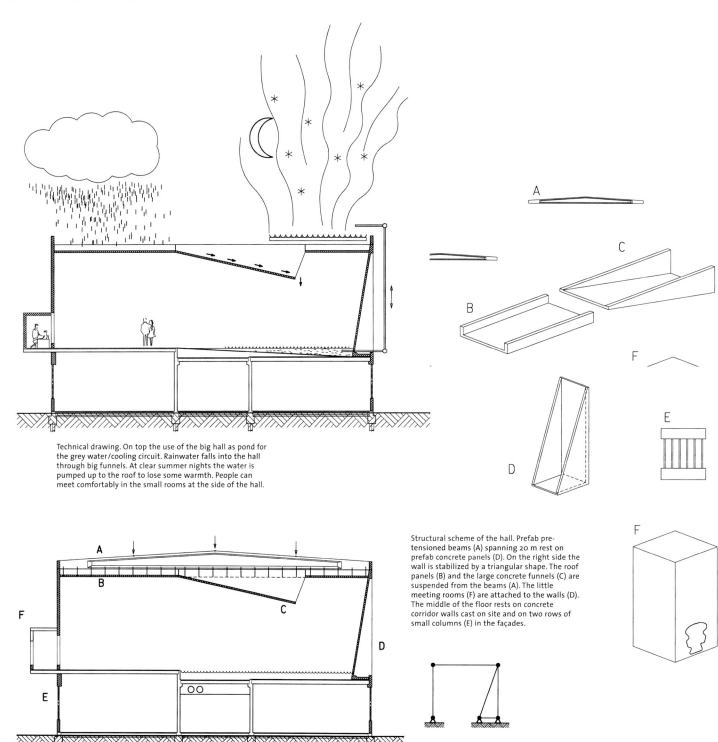

Technical drawing. On top the use of the big hall as pond for the grey water/cooling circuit. Rainwater falls into the hall through big funnels. At clear summer nights the water is pumped up to the roof to lose some warmth. People can meet comfortably in the small rooms at the side of the hall.

Structural scheme of the hall. Prefab pre-tensioned beams (A) spanning 20 m rest on prefab concrete panels (D). On the right side the wall is stabilized by a triangular shape. The roof panels (B) and the large concrete funnels (C) are suspended from the beams (A). The little meeting rooms (F) are attached to the walls (D). The middle of the floor rests on concrete corridor walls cast on site and on two rows of small columns (E) in the façades.

Small Columns

The ground floor accomodates only the labs and annexes for the lab assistants. Because of the required flexibility the architect wanted to position all columns in the façade plane. Contrary to usual practice, he also preferred a high number of small columns to a small number of big columns, for example, 300 x 300 mm columns every 7 m. This was called the concept of the "spread" column. In our design we integrated the window frame structure with the supporting column function. Combining these factors, we decided in favour of steel 100 x 100 mm cylinders, 600 mm centre-to-centre, filled with concrete and covered with fireproof paint. Since in the back part four building layers rest on these columns, it was crucial to mobilize as many favourable factors as possible, the most effective one being the clamping construction that was introduced: top and bottom of the column were clamped into a prefab element, the lower concrete beam of the façade element forming the parapet, the upper concrete beam acting as the ceiling strip. The fact that the columns were clamped reduced the buckling length to about 70 % of the normal length of the column.

The insulated glass panels were fixed straight to the steel hollow sections of the columns with an internal clamp construction. Especially when it is dark, the lit lab spaces look like open seas of light on which the rest of the rather closed building floats.

Elegant opening in one of the meeting rooms of the big hall.

Interior of the big hall.

The big pond. The rainwater falls from the funnels into a shell filled with seashells to reduce the effect of the "acid rain". Two boys stand on the flood line, which goes up and down depending on the rainfall. In rare dry periods tap water is added, while an overflow takes care of excess rainfall.

The Milkmaid Principle

The lecture rooms manifest themselves at the back of the building by an approximately 4-m-deep projection on the outside. Inside the building, the office block projects into the hall, over a distance of about 5 m. Making the first detailed sketches of the structural corridor walls we noticed these projecting parts to the left and to the right of the walls. In consultation with the architect we managed to make almost equal building weights jut out on both sides. As a consequence, the wall functions as a huge console with a concentrated tie-band in its upper part: a transverse power transmission instead of the usual bending moment transmission. We called this the milkmaid principle after the old pictures of Dutch farm girls carrying the milk in two buckets in a yoke on their shoulders. The only one who was not too pleased with this frivolous construction model was the contractor. He had to leave the tall and heavy props under the projections in place until the tie-band at the top had dried.

The non-structural columns of the restaurant, with day and/or artificial light from the top and treated air blowing in gently from the lower parts. The columns identify the space around them for a more intimate character of this large and high restaurant.

The Shotcrete Façade

Since various functional and architectural starting-points gave the Minnaert building an elongated shape, with a raised part at both ends, the façade came to determine the face of the building. Here the architect's source of inspiration was a reflection of the academic discipline located immediately behind the Minnaert building, the faculty of geology or earth sciences. Images of different surfaces of the earth such as boulders served as points of reference for the façade. Finally, the image of ripples of sand, left on the beach when the tide is low, was opted for. A slide of such ripples was projected onto the drawing of the façade, and we wondered how this could be realized. At the time the Educatorium was in full swing as well, so once again the shotcrete rocks built for a zoo made their entry. The architect was taken on a visit to this zoo, and it was decided to search for a solution along these lines.

As the shotcrete skin had to be applied to prefab concrete wall elements covered with insulation material, the suggestion was to use wire netting to make the ripples and then build the outer skin from shotcrete. But the scale of it all, was about 3,000 m²! Also the architect's dream of using coloured concrete – he wanted an earthen colour: terra-cotta – , called for intense investigative work. Moreover, all edges, corners, window-frames and gutters had to be made in shotcrete as well. From a test model with all the

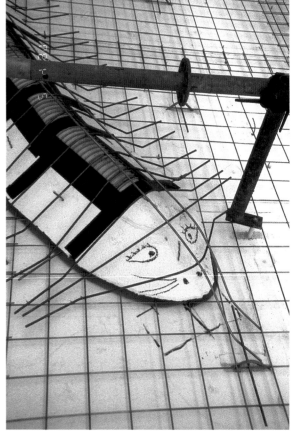

Plastic tubes and triangular elements of the polystyrene insulation for the shotcrete ribbons. A creative worker turned it into a caterpillar.

The ribbons in the shotcrete façade are merely interrupted by the window openings. The dilatation joints of the façade were integrated in the pattern of the ribbons and the position of the windows.

difficult elements, scale 1 to 1, we learned (apart from many non-feasibilities) that a layer of shotcrete coloured in the mass with a thickness of 50 mm and reinforced with a stainless steel net would be a proper solution.

A major design decision was whether or not to create a ventilated cavity. On the one hand a cavity is a perfect "damp" transport solution, on the other hand creating a cavity with shotcrete is rather a problem and very expensive, mainly because of the pressure when applying this type of concrete. Calculations by the building physics consultant showed that the prefab concrete inner wall would be damp-proof, provided the seams were taped up properly. This allowed us to apply the shotcrete directly onto the hard-press insulation. It proved possible to make shotcrete with only 10 mm of water penetration – hence no pores – so that the concrete would hardly suck up water and get dirty or freeze (and break).

For the ripples substructure, tests showed that flexible tubes fixed to the hard-press insulation with triangular fittings were the best and easiest solution. Because of the intensity of the fitting activities, the ripples remained a very expensive element, however, and were used sparsely.

Another practical point was the need for dilatations as the façade, which is approximately 150 m long, would shrink and dilate in accordance with the outside temperature. The fairly dark colour of the terra-cotta makes the surface temperature rise to about 60 or 70°C in summer. Contrasted with the minus 20°C in winter this means a temperature fluctuation of 80°C or about 150 mm expansion. This would create serious cracks. The architect suggested to let nature have its way and accept the pattern of natural cracks. This would have been acceptable if the façade had been put on in summer so that the cracks due to shrinking would have formed during the winter, but unfortunately it was to be put on in spring. It would first dilate in a non-cracked condition, possibly making pieces of concrete fall off under the influence of the compressive stress. The stainless steel reinforcement net in the middle of the shotcrete layer would not necessarily prevent this. Hence the suggestion to add a pattern of artificial dilatation joints in a grid of approximately 10 x 10 m. The dilatation lines were arranged unobtrusively in a pattern following the ripples on the surface and over and under the windows.

The façade is four years old now and looks perfect and almost new, despite all the fears of its getting dirty. The water penetration requirement of 10 mm was a major condition in this respect. All in all, it is fair to say that this large-scale implementation of shotcrete, used as a façade skin, or a (rain)coat, for a building, turned out to be a perfect new option for façades that need a touch of the three-dimensional.

Top view revealing the structural system of the roof. The big concrete beams are exposed. The architect wanted a smooth underside, while the top was to be made as simple as possible.

The only building in the world that stands on his own name. During construction the name was the first thing to appear above ground level.

The EXPO 2000 Dutch Pavilion

Computer image showing the intended appearance of the Dutch pavilion. Situated in a garden filled with flowers, the land given back to nature, the "stacked landscape" represents a view of future Holland.

The real building. Note the almost perfect match between computer image and reality.

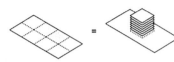

The design philosophy of the stacked landscape by MVRDV. Eight layers create free space around that can be given back to nature.

How can the achievements of technology be used to build a dignified existence with deep respect for Mother Nature? The EXPO in Hanover from June to October 2000 raised this question, and the Dutch pavilion manifested an answer with a very clear vision. In 1997 an invited competition was won by MVRDV, the architects' firm combining the talents and capacities of Winy Maas, Jacob Van Rijs and Nathalie De Vries. Their proposal was comprehensive, very innovative, intelligent and expressive of a fascinating vision. The design and its rational aspect – building in layers, putting landscapes on top of each other to meet all possible needs on a minimal surface – has become world-famous. It implied a breach with many conventions: no façade along the wide avenue where it was situated, the site split up into eight equal parts and these parts then put on top of each other: the piled-landscape concept. Visitors did not walk along a main façade, but had four façades to enter, or rather to lure them into the building.

The design also had two spiritual layers: the water balance (typically Dutch!) and the energy balance. Water on the roof and a water curtain were two aspects of the water balance, which was based on circulation and re-use. From the roof the water drips down along the water curtain to the forest, where through sprinkling and spraying the vegetation is given all the moisture it needs. Through the soil the water trickles down to the oyster, crossing it in

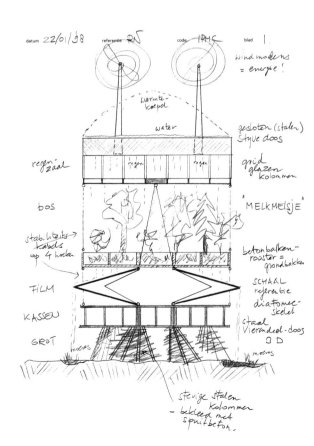

small streams to the greenhouse layer, watering the crop. The final stage leads the water down to the ground floor where reed swamps and the bacteria in them purify the water, so that it can be pumped up again to the roof and start another cycle. At the same time the building is conceived as a self-sufficient unit, with the roof used as an economically sound place for a number of windmills and additional energy coming from the bio mass in the swamps and the heat storage in the deep subsoil.

The First Structural Concept

MVRDV's competition design for the pavilion construction was still rather conceptual. All that was suggested was a simple pile of construction systems, different in each layer. After ABT had been selected as the structural consulting firm, it was up to us to translate this concept into a constructable building, in consultation with the architects.

Our approach called for solid steel columns at the bottom, genuine supports, hidden in the shape of the vaults, covered with firm wire and reinforcement steel and then turned into a cave with a layer of shotcrete. On top of these supports there was to be a strong and solid Vierendeel box with a three-dimensional effect. A Vierendeel girder, named after the Belgian engineer Vierendeel, is a grid without diagonals. By making the Vierendeel girders run in two perpendicular directions and using the floor and the bottom of this storey we were able to create what we called the 3D Vierendeel box. One of the structural discoveries of this experimental pavilion is that this principle works well.

The box accommodated the greenhouse layer, on top of which came the cinema hall, the oyster. The strong external calcium skeleton of the diatoms is a well-known phenomenon in biology, and surely there had to be a way to imitate this beautiful skeleton in ferroconcrete. On top of the oyster the forest-floor layer, a mutually perpendicular grid of concrete beams, about 1.5 m high, made the soil tanks for the trees an integral part of the construction. Here the architects wanted no columns, just pure nature, which was going to be difficult with the layer on top of the forest. We suggested the "milkmaid" principle: like the girls that used to balance two buckets of milk with a yoke on their shoulders, the building would be supported at a central point in the middle and stability ensured by taut cables at the four corners. The oyster layer was stabilized in the same manner. Balancing on top of the forest level was the rain hall. Glass combines perfectly with water, so glass columns were suggested for this level. Earlier ABT studies into this subject made the use of these very special structural elements possible. On top of the rain hall came a solid steel tank for the roof pond, with the windmills clamped into this steel box.

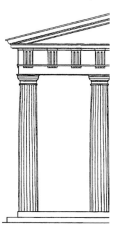

Columns in the Dorian style of a Greek temple. The vertical stripes, the cannelures, remind of the bark of oak trees originally used as columns in the first generation of Greek temples.

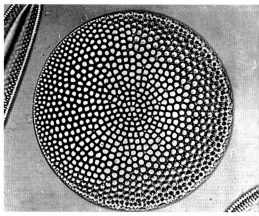

The chalk skeleton of a diatom. This was the inspiration for the structure of the cinema hall, the load-bearing oyster.

The first structural sketch of the original design. A stiff one-story layer in a Vierendeel structure rests on concrete hills. On top of this a cable-stayed shell, housing the cinema, followed by the forest on the third floor with a single cone-shaped column in the centre. On top of this a steel box, inside it a grid of glass columns supporting the water layer on top of the pavilion. Windmills on top provide electricity.

The proposal for the structure at the end of the final design stage. A corrugated concrete slab cast on stabilized sand hills carries a 3 D Vierendeel box housing the agricultural exhibition. The Vierendeel box carries the oyster layer. On top of this the load-bearing oak tree trunks of the forest layer. Using the masts of the windmills as columns, a concrete shell hangs between them. The island in the middle of the shell that is to be filled with water serves as structural stiffening. Water is constantly pumped up, and flowing over the edge of the concrete shell, it creates a water curtain.

Finite-Element-Method computer image of the structural basis of the oyster that had to carry a large part of the building. The tensile steel ring in the centre consists of a massive steel section of about 1.5 by 0.5 m.

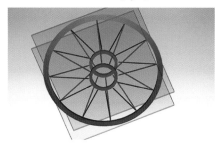

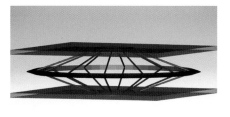

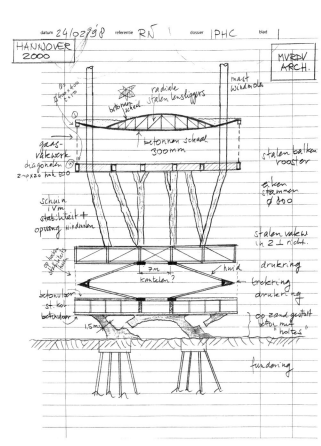

The Second Structural Concept

Unfortunately, some of these elements found no favour in the eyes of the client and especially the exhibition curators. Rain in a hall did not sound very appealing to them. There were also budget-related doubts about some parts of the design, like the "milkmaid" construction. Therefore, alternatives were studied that would not give rise to such objections.

The question of the rain hall was solved by opting for a rain curtain along the façade. The water falls over the edge creating a mysterious moment where the building ends for the visitor on the roof. The water curtain was integrated into the construction by a so-called "wire" truss along the edges, a truss with not just a few diagonals, but a great many small, intersecting ones, serving as a "canvas" for the water to run over.

The water on the roof was collected in a dish, the most economical solution for the purpose of containing a big quantity of water. Because of the heavy weight of the water this dish could be loaded for traction only. This required, however, that the edges had to be very stiff and very well supported; at this point the steel wire grid of the truss inserted into the surface of the façade (or the rain curtain) came in conveniently. But how to make a water dish starting from a square? The architectural design required that the only thing to be seen on the roof was to be water. No problem for a circular plain, but more difficult

The structural trees under construction.

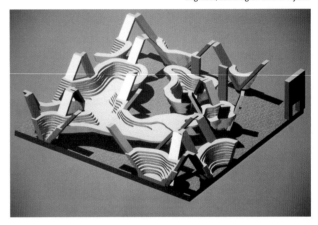

The computer model used by MVRDV and ABT to incorporate the tilted columns in the concrete dunes. It was sent back and forth till both parties, the architect and the structural engineer, could agree on the layout.

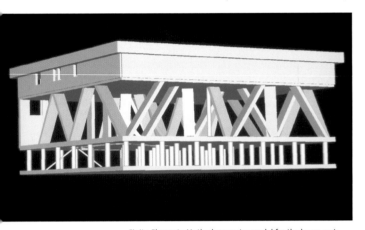

Finite-Elements-Method computer model for the lower part made out of cast concrete. It was intended to be re-used and to be able to carry ten layers of office building.

The realized structure. The corrugated concrete dunes are made of shotcrete covering inclined columns. On top of the dunes the concrete 3 D Vierendeel box. On top of that a flowerpot layer meant to hold the roots of the forest on the next layer. In the forest the oak tree trunks act as structural columns. Above the forest a steel structure housing the cinema hall. On the roof of this hall half a meter of water, faint memory of the 3-m-deep concrete shell. On top of the pavilion six windmills and an earth-clad island holding the VIP room with a silver ceiling inside.

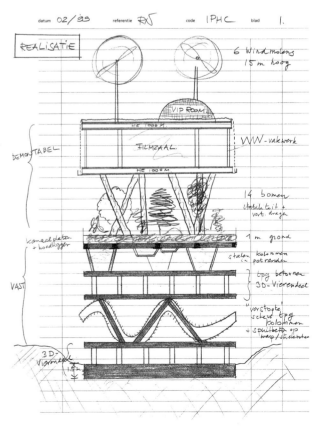

for a square one: the corners would hold little to no water. We suggested to load a flat square plate with the water pressure (in the computer) and make the ensuing deformation the starting-point for the shape of the dish. In this way it would always be filled with water and have 3 m of water at its lowest point.

The milkmaid principle for the forest layer was too dominant with its central cone. So how could we construct a forest? With the help of trees, was the proper answer. The first column ever used by man surely must have been a treetrunk. An intact treetrunk has the right strength: it has not only withstood many a storm in its long existence, but also the fibres have been left untouched and intact, while a plank or beam is disturbed in its fibre coherence because of the sawing. So we decided to opt for the most primitive column: the treetrunk.

The fine diatom shells planned for the oyster were not able to cope with the many visitor entrances, passages and escape routes required by modern fire-safety regulations. The alternative was a traction and compression analogous to the construction we had built for the Feyenoord soccer stadium in Rotterdam. In this system, diagonals direct the vertical load to a horizontal floating ring. The ring would be pushed aside by the force in any given diagonal, but because of the spatial effect the respective opposed diagonal would be pushed in the opposite direction, so that as a result the horizontal power, passed on through the ring, ensures a balance and makes the tensile ring float. Downward diagonals pass the forces on to the construction below. At the point of entry and exit a compression ring warrants the stability of the construction.

The ring system would be placed on top of the 3D Vierendeel system, which in turn rested on concrete vaults – now adopting the more poetical name of "dunes" – consisting of a 1.5 m layer of reinforced concrete, poured onto hills of stabilized sand to be removed when the concrete had hardened.

All parts were calculated and dimensioned by ABT; the first cost estimate amounted to a total of 7,350,000 Euro. Unfortunately, the budget for the construction was only 4,700,000 Euro. So this meant that we had to cut down our ambition. The client, who was not completely satisfied, suggested that we rationalize the construction. The architects were asked to indicate some priority in the various construction systems.

The concrete dunes under construction; the tilted columns disappear under a wire mesh and shotcrete.

Foot detail of the structural trees. Strong men connect the treetrunk to the structure of the floor.

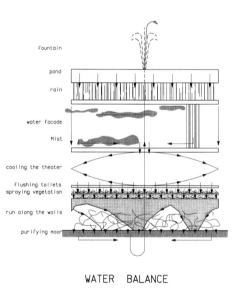

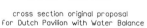

WATER BALANCE

cross section original proposal
for Dutch Pavilion with Water Balance

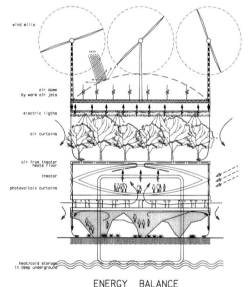

ENERGY BALANCE

_____ wind/air   cross section original proposal
_·_·_·_ warmth   for Dutch Pavilion with Energy Balance
------ electricity

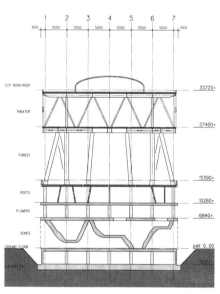

CROSS SECTION BUILDING

Third: the Final Design

The architects' answer was surprising: "Let us eliminate the most expensive element and replace it with a more rational layer." The costliest part was the oyster, which was a pity, since this element would have been very innovative from a structural point of view. The oyster layer was replaced by a replica of the layer below (later this layer was turned into the basement layer). But the architects also suggested a new layer, the pot or root layer, to be introduced below the tree layer in order to expose the roots of the forest on top. This is how the root pots were born. We imagined these beautiful visual elements to be prefab concrete pots, made on site and then lifted on top of the greenhouse layer where they were to serve as support construction for the forest layer.

This approach was influenced by the desire to build in detachable parts from the greenhouse layer upwards. The sustainable building, a major topic of this World Exhibition, was translated into combining a firm foundation, reaching to the top of the greenhouse layer, with detachable parts above. The intention was that the upper part could be re-used after the exhibition at another location, presumably in the Netherlands, while ten office layers could be put on top of the foundation for a re-use of that part after the end of EXPO 2000.

Sustainable water cycle. Water pumped up by the energy of the windmills creates a fountain in the pond on top of the building. The water flows through holes in the "floor" of the pond into the "rainy" exhibition room and then continues as "rain" in the living forest. After that the water flows over the skin of the oyster cooling it. Then it becomes rain once again, in the agricultural exhibition, and finally drips over the concrete dunes into a swamp where it is purified by water plants before being pumped up again.

Energy Balance. Windmills and photo-voltaic cells provide energy for the water cycle and create a "heat" dome on top of the building. Here hot air jets blow away the cold as well as the rain. A natural ventilation concept is installed in the oyster holding the cinema hall. A warm and cold storage in the deep underground allows the building to use the coldness of winter in summer and vice versa.

Fourth: the Realization

While digging the basement and the foundation, the plans for the structural work were rounded off and put out to tender, but still the lowest tender did not meet the budget. So more cuts had to be made, resulting in Draconian interventions. The beautiful steel hanging dish was cancelled because of its many expensive joints, in spite of its minimal use of steel; the floating VIP island was turned into a VIP house and the 3 m of water depth were reduced to 30 cm. A steel beam grid with channel plates replaced the original roof construction. The prefab pots were replaced by columns in the pot walls; later the shape of the pots was created with stucco. And the layer of dunes was replaced by slanting columns with a shotcrete skin as an aesthetic cover.

In February/March 1999 the big adventure was about to start: the building of the Hanover pavilion.

Construction: Concrete Layers

The three bottom layers of the building are made of concrete, cast on site, the foundation is also made of concrete.

A 1,300-mm-thick concrete foundation plate distributes the loads at ground level. Together with the floor of the groundlevel layer and the columns of the basement it forms the first of two 3D Vierendeel constructions in the

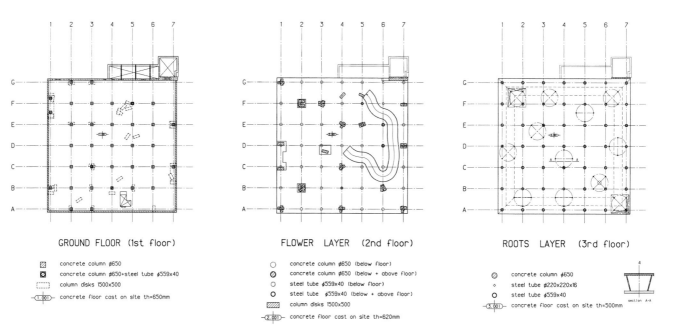

GROUND FLOOR (1st floor)

⊠ concrete column ⌀650
⊠ concrete column ⌀650+steel tube ⌀559x40
▭ column disks 1500x500
(1.001) concrete floor cast on site th=650mm

FLOWER LAYER (2nd floor)

○ concrete column ⌀650 (below floor)
⊘ concrete column ⌀650 (below + above floor)
○ steel tube ⌀559x40 (below floor)
○ steel tube ⌀559x40 (below + above floor)
▨ column disks 1500x500
(2.001) concrete floor cast on site th=620mm

ROOTS LAYER (3rd floor)

⊘ concrete column ⌀650
◇ steel tube ⌀220x220x16
○ steel tube ⌀559x40
(3.001) concrete floor cast on site th=500mm

section A-A

lower part of the building. Here this construction ensures optimum distribution of the pointed loads caused by the slanting columns integrated into the dunes. A Vierendeel girder takes its stiffness from joints (with bending strength) between the horizontal styles and the vertical bars. As there are no diagonal bars, this construction has the advantage (when compared to a grid) that there are fewer obstructions in the space between the styles (the floors in this case). But since bending is a less efficient way to absorb forces, each girder must have a much heavier construction compared to a truss with diagonals. As a consequence, the columns are 650 x 650 mm in size and the ground floor plate is 600 mm thick.

In the dune landscape between ground and first floor, inclined columns act like a skeleton in a shape that passes the forces on to the basement. The landscape consists of two layers of shotcrete with a hollow space in between, conveying the impression of a massive plate with as little material as possible. In this way a clear distinction is made between the design element and the support structure, while at the same time the positions of the inclined columns (1,500 x 500 mm in size) and the dune dips/tops are closely related: the dunes form the lines that connect the points touching the floor below (the dune dips) and the floor above (the dune tops). Through their close cooperation the structural engineers and the architect found a geometry which met both the constructional and aesthetic/functional demands.

The flowerpot layer. For the big trees large pots were created, smaller plants got smaller, suspended pots. Later during the design process it proved that a 1-m-thick layer of earth is sufficient for a real forest. The pots were then used for several other functions like a disabled toilet, a machine room and an exhibition space.

The second 3D Vierendeel girder was formed by the floor plates above the dunes and the greenhouse layer, together with the columns in the greenhouse layer. Again the advantage of less obstruction between the columns is paid for by a heavier construction. On this floor the columns are round and have a diameter of 650 mm. The upper floor is 500 mm thick.

For a proper understanding of the interplay of forces the four lower levels were fed into a 3D model of an FEM calculation program at an early stage. This model could then be used in the design stage to examine the influence of any geometry changes on the power absorption in the entire construction. When the architects shifted dune tops and dips about, column positions were shifted in the computer model until they had reached their ideal shape from a structural and architectural perspective. In the building stage the same computer model could be used to determine the dimensioning of the reinforcement in plates/disks and columns.

Invisible to the visitor, the transition from the massive concrete construction to the detachable steel construction takes place on the pot layer. The lower floor plate still belongs to the massive part. The upper floor of the pot layer consists of channel plates with integrated hood beams and is supported by slender tubular columns or thick steel columns at places where high pointed loads are introduced by the trees above. The columns are concealed in the walls of the pots which house functional facilities. The horizontal loads on this level are absorbed by the efficient implementation of tensile diagonals. The 2 x 2 wind bracings located at the corners of the building are completely hidden in the walls of the pots as well. So there is a limited obstruction of space.

Construction: Steel Layers
Forest Floor

From the top of the root layer the construction is carried out in steel, which is combined with channel plate floors. The concept of the construction of the forest layer was heavily influenced by the horizontal forces introduced by the slanting tree columns. These forces must be linked and balanced by tensile and compression bands in the floor. The floor consists of an irregular grid of THQ-girders, tubular-shaped girders with a wide bottom flange, on which the channel plates rest. The THQ-girders rest on slender pendulum columns, which have been distributed rather irregularly over this layer in order to integrate them in the structural pot walls. 14 trees serve as columns, 8 of them slanted to ensure the stability of this 14-m-high level.

Theatre Floor

On the theatre hall layer, a horizontal floor-disk effect is achieved by steel diagonals made of tubes (round 193.7 mm), combined with the steel beam grid of the floor (HE1000A, HE1000B and HE1000M) to form the actual floor grid. This grid is essential for conducting the horizontal wind forces to the slanting trees and for creating the balance for the horizontal forces. The steel beams of this floor are supported by the 14 structural trees of the forest layer. Eight of them are inclined so as to transport the horizontal forces to the floor of the forest layer without any additional vertical bracings in the forest.

The steel beam grid of the theatre hall floor was combined with a 200-mm-thick concrete channel plate floor. This combination of steel girders and channel plates has a number of advantages. The steel grid floor itself could be assembled in three parts on the building site at ground level, these were then lifted onto the columns (trees), where the horizontal and permanent joints were added and the channel plates laid. After the end of EXPO 2000 the construction could be disassembled in reverse order and all parts of it re-used at another location.

The forest on the third floor. The two V-shaped inclined oak treetrunks contribute to the stability. The lights in the ceiling enabled natural growth also in the centre of the building.

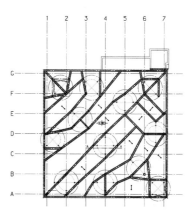

FOREST LAYER (4th floor)

- steel/concrete beams
- span hollow core slabs th=400, screed th=100
- steel tube ⌀220x220x16
- steel tube ⌀559x25
- hollow core slabs th=400

section A-A

The design team checking oak trees in the Ommen forest. On the left: Jacob van Rijs (MVRDV).

Roof

The same holds true for the roof-floor construction. The reduction of the water level on the roof to 30 cm made it possible to use here a symmetrical grid floor as well. It consists of steel girders (HE900A, HE900B and HE900M) which rest on 12 prefab concrete columns (500 mm, round) integrated into the walls of the theatre hall and on four steel cylinder profile trusses in the façade. The 260 mm channel plates have a maximum span of 6,000 mm. The intended horizontal disk effect is created by stiff joints between the steel girders. These joints lead the horizontal forces to the trusses in the façade, which function as vertical disks.

The vertical façade trusses rest on the projection of the floor of the theatre hall. Therefore, it was essential to calculate the two floors together to determine the distribution of the forces. Depending on the stiffnesses selected, the grids would no longer rest on the floor of the theatre hall, but would rather suspend from it.

Construction: Treetrunk Columns

When the decision was made to use real treetrunks as columns in the forest layer, we did not realize from the start that we were going back to the very beginnings of architecture. The columns used in the first temples built

Top detail of the structural trees. One can see the elastic placed in between. Notice the two parts of the steel connection : one steel connection to the treetrunk and one steel connection to the structure of the floor on top.

Detail of the tensioned fabric over which the water curtain flows. When the wind increases to values above 7 Beaufort the water curtain has to be turned off.

THEATER LAYER (5th floor)

⌀193,7x8,0 (stabilition braces)
HE1000-beam
span hollow core slabs th=200
concrete column ⌀500
tree trunk (oak) ⌀800 (average)
hollow core slabs th=200

by mankind must have been treetrunks. In the woods, the sacred place, the altar, was surrounded by a row of trees. Gradually the trees, as treetrunks that hold up the roof, became real columns, and later the perishable wood was replaced by stone.

Our initial, exploratory calculations showed that we needed a total of some 14 treetrunks with a length of approximately 14 m and an average diameter of about 800 mm. As wind bracings are far from natural in a wood, it was decided to add stability to this layer by making a number of trees tilt, in pairs, and create a support system which would be able to absorb horizontal forces. We opted for a Dutch tree, the oak, mainly because oak wood has a lot of supporting power and is rather immune to the elements. Another important factor for the architects was its beautiful bark.

A tree of the required size is about 200 years old. They would have been fairly expensive to buy from the timber industry and could not be delivered in the necessary quantities. Enquiries with the forestry administration led to the impression that we would have to buy the trees not in one single batch but in pairs or even as single trees. Moreover, the quality of the trunks turned out to be determined very much by the health of the wood, so that the trees had to be examined carefully with regard to history of growth and environment. Fortunately, in the summer of 1998, we found what we needed in a forest

Interaction between the corrugated concrete dunes (with slanting columns hidden inside) and the 3 D Vierendeel box of the agricultural exhibition layer.

near the town of Ommen. Circumstances there also helped us avoid a delicate matter. How does one justify the fact that beautiful 200-year-old oak trees are made to carry a pavilion that is meant to be sustainable? The Ommen forest, the Laarbos, was about 200 years old, but the trees had been planted too close together so that the wood was on the verge of choking and could no longer regenerate. It was necessary to make the Laarbos see some light and gain some air. The trees were left to hibernate and were going to be cut down in March 1999, just before the spring flow of juices started.

In the meantime we discussed things with the "Prüfingenieur" in charge of the project, for in Germany all calculations and all building materials must be approved. His first reaction was one of utter disbelief. Surely this was not possible: using whole trees that had no "approved" label in a building visited by so many people! There was, however, a willingness to engage in further investigations as to the quality of the forest as a whole, an appearance-based selection of the trees, a drill test performed on each selected tree and lab tests for strength, elasticity modulus and degree of moisture. The latter factor was especially important, in order to be able to reduce shrinkage and the damage by insects and their larvae. An important, and for us favourable, fact was that a tree does not shrink lengthwise, but only crossways.

In March 1999 the trees were felled, an impressive event which makes you feel a bit guilty as the human being responsible for the action. After testing there was a whole series of objections to several of the trees felled. Consequently, they were rejected, new ones were selected and tested, but after a month we had already cut down 39 trees. We had to stop in the Laarbos. Only three of the felled trees were perfect, of six we had our doubts and the rest was not fit for a pavilion. Finally the rejected trees were used for carpeting, and we had to start looking for oak trees all over again.

A new suggestion was to use azobé trunks from the tropical rainforest. They were easily available, not expensive and beautiful. And had not Surinam in the past been part of the Netherlands? The emotional aversion to tropical hardwood and the boring nature of the peeled azobé trunks were too much of an obstacle, though. Instead, we went back to the lumber yards and travelled all over Europe searching for beautiful, tall oaks. After wandering through Germany and France we ended up in Denmark, where on the island of Seeland good oaks could be bought at a reasonable price. But in the meantime we were faced with trees in full foliage, the wood of which had turned moist because the juices had started to flow. Fortunately, forestry experts knew that moisture evaporates from the trees through the leaves, so that after felling and performing the drill tests the trees were just left on the floor, with all their leaves.

Finally, the proper E-modulus, measured for each oak, was fed into the 3D computer model, in order to compute the distribution of forces and the deformations with the proper stiffness ratios. For construction a steel plate would be firmly fitted to each treetrunk. On this steel plate the first part of a shoe was mounted, the other part of the shoe was fixed to the floor or ceiling of the building. The two parts are separated by an elastomere cushion, for each treetrunk is a pendulum bar, with a hinge at both ends. Since each treetrunk is only subjected to compressive loads (even in storms and during construction), the cushions can distribute all eccentric loads and differences in temperature (i.e. the resulting differences in expansion) over several columns, which means that uneven distributions of column loads are avoided.

On 17 November 1999 we were quite relieved to hear that the treetrunks had officially been approved of by the "Prüfingenieur", and just before Christmas 1999 there were two Dutch oaks, one Dutch beech and eleven Danish oaks mounted on the building site of the Dutch pavilion. After about 6000 years of technological advance there were treetrunks again in a manmade building – the difference being that these had been turned inside out and become a virtual part of advanced computer calculations in which they were exposed to all kinds of possible and impossible combinations of forces.

The roof of the Dutch pavilion with the water, the mast of a windmill and the "earth" island that housed the VIP room.

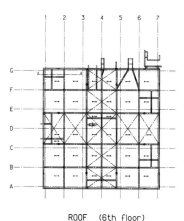

ROOF (6th floor)

L100x100x12 (steel angle)
HE900-beam
span hollow core slabs th=200
concrete column φ500
hollow core slabs th=200

APPENDIX

Project Data

Glass Beams

Project **Glass Pavilion for the Sonsbeek Art Exhibition – Arnhem**
project demolished
Completed 1986
Client Stichting Sonsbeek Beelden Arnhem
Architect Benthem en Crouwel Architecten Amsterdam
Structural engineer ABT – Arnhem/Delft
Contractor BAM – Arnhem
Glass producer Betuwse Glashandel-Tiel

Project **Glass Roof for the European Patent Office – Leidschendam**
Completed project not realized (1992)
Client European Patent Organisation – München
Architect Neutelings en Roodbeen Architecten – Rotterdam
Structural Engineer ABT – Arnhem/Delft

Project **Glass Roof for a Renovated Office Building – Budapest**
Address Andrássy út 20
Completed 1994
Client Nationale Nederlanden Vastgoed – Den Haag
Architect Mecanoo Architecten; Erick van Egeraat – Delft
Structural engineer ABT – Arnhem/Delft
Contractor CFE – Brussels
Glass producer Portal – Brussels

Project **Glass Footbridge – Rotterdam**
Address Watertorenseweg 336
Completed 1994
Client Kraaijvanger Urbis – Rotterdam
Architect Kraaijvanger Urbis; Dirk Jan Postel – Rotterdam
Structural engineer ABT – Arnhem/Delft
Glass producer Alverre – Almelo

Project **Glass Footbridge – Arnhem**
Address Schelmseweg 85
Completed 1996
Client Burgers' Zoo – Arnhem
Architect Wiegerinck Architecten Arnhem
Structural engineer ABT – Arnhem/Delft
Contractor BAM – Arnhem
Glass producer Saint Roch – Maarssen

Project **Large Glass Beam – Amsterdam**
Completed project not realized (1998)
Client Zwitserleven – Amstelveen
Architect De Architekten Cie. - Amsterdam
Structural engineer ABT – Arnhem/Delft
Contractor Ballast Nedam – Amstelveen
Glass producer Octatube – Delft

Project **Glass Stairway for a Museum – Zwolle**
Address Stedelijk museum; Voorstraat 34
Completed 1998
Client Municipality Zwolle
Architect Van der Belt & Partners Architecten – Zwolle
Structural engineer ABT – Arnhem/Delft
Contractor Van Beverwijk – Zwolle
Glass producer Alverre – Almelo

Project **Canopies – Nijmegen**
Address Stationsplein
Completed 1999
Client Municipality Nijmegen
Architect Cepezed - Delft
Structural engineer ABT – Arnhem/Delft
Contractor Nijssen Bouw – 's-Hertogenbosch
Glass producer Betuwse Glashandel - Tiel

Project **Glass Bridge for Floriade 2002 – Hoofddorp**
Address Hoofdstraat
Completed project not realized
Client Municipality Haarlemmermeer
Architect Joris Lüchinger – Rotterdam
Structural engineer ABT – Arnhem/Delft

Glass Floors

Project **Indoor Floor for a Clubhouse – Arnhem**
Address Bakenbergseweg 256a
Completed 1995
Client Hockeyclub Upward-Arnhem
Architect Frank Roodbeen – Amsterdam
Structural Engineer ABT – Arnhem/Delft
Contractor Van Aalderen Bouw – Doorwerth
Glass Producer Alverre-Almelo

Project **Indoor Floor for the Educatorium – Utrecht**
Address Leuvenlaan 4, De Uithof
Completed 1997
Client University of Utrecht
Architect OMA – Rotterdam
Structural Engineer ABT – Arnhem/Delft
Contractor BAM – Bunnik
Glass Producer Van den Heuvel Glas – Schiedam

Project **Outdoor Glass Deck – Nijmegen**
Address Stationsplein
Completed 1998
Client Municipality Nijmegen
Architect Cepezed – Delft
Structural Engineer ABT Arnhem/Delft
Contractor Nijssen Bouw – Rosmalen
Glass Producer Betuwse Glashandel – Tiel

Project **Labyrinth "Hildegard von Bingen" – Ruurlo**
Completed project not realized at time of writing
Client State of Gelderland – Arnhem/Bea Snijders-Verheul – Ruurlo
Architect Hildegard von Bingen/Father Henri Bodaerts
Structural Engineer ABT – Arnhem/Delft

Project **Glass Stairs – Arnhem**
Address Eusebiusplein
Completed 2001
Client City of Arnhem
Architect AGS Architecten en Planners, Heerlen/Arnhem
Structural engineer ABT – Arnhem/Delft
Contractor Trebbe Aannemingsmaatschappi – Eschede
Glass producer Alverre, Almelo

Glass Columns

Project **Glass Truss Elements for an Office Building – Amstelveen**
Address Burgemeester Rijnderslaan 7
Completed 1996
Client Zwitserleven Insurance Company Amstelveen
Architect Architecten Cie – Amsterdam
Structural Engineer ABT – Arnhem/Delft
Contractor Ballast Nedam – Amstelveen
Glass Producer Octatube – Delft

Project **Spiral Staircase in the ABT-Office – Arnhem**
Completed project not realized at time of writing
Client ABT – Arnhem/Delft
Structural Engineer ABT – Arnhem/Delft

Project **Composite Column (Concept) – Utrecht**
Completed project not realized
Client University of Utrecht
Architect Wiel Arets Architects & Assiociates – Maastricht
Structural Engineer ABT – Arnhem/Delft

Project **Variations on a Column – Holten and Seoul**
Completed Holten: 1993, not realized
Seoul: 1997, not realized
Architect OMA – Rotterdam
Structural Engineer ABT – Arnhem/Delft

Project **Case Study: A Realized Glass Column – Saint-Germain-en-Laye**
Address Rue Léon Désoyé
Completed 1994
Client Saint-Germain-en-Laye
Architect Brunet et Saunier
Structural Engineer O.T.H./Alto – M. Malinowski
Glass Producer Saint Roch – Paris

Project **Tularosa Glass Tower Project**
Completed project not realized at time of writing
Client Patti O'Neal – Berlin
Artist Patti O'Neal – Berlin
Structural Engineer ABT – Arnhem/Delft

Project **A Glass Column Solution, ABT-Office – Arnhem**
Address Arnhemsestraatweg 358 – Velp
Completed project not realized at time of writing
Client ABT – Arnhem
Structural Engineer ABT – Arnhem/Delft

Project **Glass Beam for Conservatory – Leiden**
Adress Hooglandse Kerkgracht 29, Leiden
Completed 2002
Architect B & D Architecten – Leiden/Oosterbeek
Structural engineer ABT – Arnhem/Delft
Contractor Du Prie Bouw en Ontwikkeling – Leiden
Glass producer Van den Heuvel Glas, Schiedam

Project **Supercolumn (Concept)**
Structural Engineer ABT – Arnhem/Delft
Completed project not realized (1996)

Glass Façades

Project	**Glass Façade for Educatorium Restaurant – Utrecht**
Address	Leuvenlaan 4 – De Uithof
Completed	1997
Client	University of Utrecht
Architect	OMA – Rotterdam
Structural Engineer	ABT – Arnhem/Delft
Contractor	BAM – Bunnik
Glass Producer	Blitta – Venray

Project	**Glass Façade for Natural Museum – Rotterdam**
Address	West Zeedijk 345
Completed	1997
Client	Municipality Rotterdam
Architect	Erick van Egeraat Arch. & Ass. – Rotterdam
Structural Engineer	ABT – Arnhem/Delft
Contractor	HBG – Rotterdam
Glass Producer	Veromco – Soest

Project	**Experimental School Façade – Heerlen**
Address	Nieuwe Eijckholt 300
Completed	1998
Client	Hogeschool Limburg – Heerlen
Architect	AGS – Heerlen
Structural Engineer	ABT – Arnhem/Delft
Contractor	BAM/Van der Linden – Eindhoven
Glass Producer	Van der Heuvel Glas – Schiedam

Project	**'Liberation' Carillon – Den Haag**
Completed	project not realized
Client	Committee 50 Years Liberation
Architect	UN Studio; Van Berkel en Bos arch. – Amsterdam
Structural Engineer	ABT – Arnhem/Delft

Project	**Rock-Stabilized Façade Design for EXPO 2000 Pavilion**
Completed	project (this part) not realized
Architect	MVRDV – Rotterdam
Structural Engineer	ABT – Arnhem/Delft

Project	**Façade Support Systems for University Libary – Utrecht**
Completed	project (this part) not realized
Client	University of Utrecht
Architect	Wiel Arets – Maastricht
Structural Engineer	ABT – Arnhem/Delft

Project	**Glass-Walled House – Talus du Temple / Avallon**
Completed	2001
Client	private person
Architect	Dirk Jan Postel – Rotterdam
Structural engineer	ABT – Arnhem/Delft
Contractor and glass producer	Alverre – Almelo

Project	**Casa da Musica – Porto**
Address	Praca de Mouzinho de Albuquerque – Porto
Completed	2004
Architect	OMA – Rotterdam
Local Architect	ANC Aquitectos- Atelier Novais Carvalho – Porto
Structural Engineer	Ove Arup & Partners - London
Local structural engineer	AFA – Consultores de Engenharia – Porto
Glass producer	Cricursa – Barcelona

Other Glass Walls

Project	**Glass Wall for Educatorium Auditorium – Utrecht**
Address	Leuvenlaan 4 – de Uithof
Completed	1997
Client	University of Utrecht
Architect	OMA – Rotterdam
Structural Engineer	ABT – Arnhem/Delft
Contractor	BAM Utiliteitsbouw – Bunnik
Glass Producer	Van den Heuvel Glas – Schiedam

Project	**Glass House – Leerdam**
Completed	project not realized
Client	Robert Winkel/Marco van Henssen – Rotterdam
Architect	Robert Winkel/Marco van Henssen – Rotterdam
Structural Engineer	ABT – Arnhem/Delft

Project	**Glass House – Leerdam**
Completed	2001
Client	Centraal Woningbeheer – Leerdam
Architect	Kruunenberg/van der Erven Architecten – Amsterdam
Structural Engineer	ABT – Arnhem/Delft (first phase of design)
	Van Rijn en Partners – Roelofarendsveen
Glass Producer	BV Radix & Veerman – Woerden
	Saint Gobain Glass – Veenendaal

Project	**Aquarium – Amsterdam**
Address	Plantage Kerklaan 40
Completed	1996 and 2001
Client	Artis Zoo – Amsterdam
Architect	Architectengroep – Amsterdam
Structural Engineer	ABT – Arnhem/Delft
Contractor	J. Kneppers bv – Amsterdam

Project	**Waterwall Concept for Eco-House – Diest**
Completed	project not realized
Architect	META Architecten – Antwerpen
Structural Engineer	ABT – Arnhem/Delft

Project	**Retaining Wall Concept and Transparent Dyke Concept**
Completed	project not realized
Structural Engineer	ABT – Arnhem/Delft

Project	**Flexible Dyke-Top Concept – Deventer**
Completed	project not realized
Structural Engineer	ABT – Arnhem/Delft

Project	**Glass Windshields – Nijmegen**
Address	Stationsplein
Completed	1998
Client	Municipality Nijmegen
Architect	Cepezed – Delft
Structural Engineer	ABT – Arnhem/Delft
Contractor	Nijssen Bouw bv – Rosmalen
Glass Producer	Betuwse Glashandel – Tiel

Glass Roofs

Project	**Dutch Pavilion for the EXPO 1998 – Lisbon**
	project demolished
Completed	1998
Client	Stichting Nederland Wereld Tentoonstellingen 's-Gravenhage
Architect	Quist Wintermans arch. – Rotterdam
Structural Engineer	ABT – Arnhem/Delft
Glass Producer	Oskomera – Deurne

Project	**Glass Dome, Tower of London**
Completed	project not realized
Client	Tower of London
Architect	Mecanoo – Delft
Structural Engineer	ABT – Arnhem/Delft

Project	**Corrugated Glass Roof for Galleria – Rotterdam**
Address	Kop van Zuid
Completed	project not realized in this shape
Architect	Zwarts & Jansma – Amsterdam
Structural Engineer	ABT – Arnhem/Delft

Project	**Glass Cone – Zwolle**
Address	Eekwal 8
Completed	1995 – 1996
Client	Notary Duret/Steenhoven – Zwolle
Architect	ir. R.P. Moritz Architect – Zwolle
Structural Engineer	ABT – Arnhem/Delft
Glass Producer	Alverre – Almelo

Project	**Awning Shopping Mall – Hengelo**
Address	Woon- en winkelcentrum de Brink
Completed	1998
Client	ING Vastgoed – Den Haag
Architect	Peter Wilson/Julia Bolles-Münster
Structural Engineer	ABT – Arnhem/Delft
Contractor	Thomasson Dura – Hengelo
Glass Producer	Eykelkamp – Goor

Project	**Water Roof, City Theatre – Almere**
Completed	project not realized
Client	Municipality of Almere
Architect	Wiel Arets – Maastricht
Structural Engineer	ABT – Arnhem/Delft

Project	**Glass Roof Concept for University Library – Utrecht**
Completed	project (this part) not realized
Client	University of Utrecht
Architect	Wiel Arets – Maastricht
Structural Engineer	ABT – Arnhem/Delft

Project	**Mobile Glass Pavilion – Rotterdam**
Completed	project not realized
Client	Rotterdam 2001 Culturele Hoofdstad
Architect	Kraayvanger Urbis – Rotterdam
Structural Engineer	ABT – Arnhem/Delft
Glass Producer	Alverre – Almelo

Project	**Structural Skylight Concept for the University of Venice**
Completed	project not realized
Architect	NoW Here Architects – Amsterdam
	(Guiseppe Mantia; Karl Amann)
Structural Engineer	ABT – Arnhem/Delft

Credits

All illustrations were provided by the author.
Photo credits are given where other copyright holders were made
known to the publisher:

Wiel Arets Architects & Associates, Maastricht: 95 (computer model)
Jordi Bernardo/Actar: 6
Rie Cramer: 10
Bram van der Heijden / Kraayvanger Urbis, Rotterdam: 29 bottom (photo)
Fas Keuzenkamp, Pijnacker; 15 (photo), 118 (photo)
Kruunenberg/van der Erven Architecten, Amsterdam: Cover, 103
Jannes Linders: 28 top (photo)
Joris Lüchinger, Rotterdam: 42 f. (all pictures of glass bridge are made
on computer)
Guiseppe Mantia, Venice, Karl Amann, Stuttgart: 138 (pictures and drawings)
Mecanoo Architects, Delft: 24 (drawing and photo of model), 125
Rob Moritz, Zwolle: 130f. (photo)
MVRDV, Rotterdam: 140 right, 154
Harry Noback, Apeldoorn: 37 top (photo)
OMA, Rotterdam: 70 bottom, 71 bottom, 101
Dirk Jan Postel / Kraayvanger Urbis Architecten, Rotterdam: 136 f.
(computer images and construction drawings)
Christian Richters, Münster: 96 f. (all photos of Avalon House)
Dario Scagliola & Stijn Brakkee: 150, 151 middle, 153 top
Imre Scany/Studio Scany, Deventer: 32 (photo of model)
Vladimir Suchov, in: M. Gappoev, R. Graefe, O. Pertschi (Ed.),
V.G. Suchov 1853 – 1939. Die Kunst der sparsamen Konstruktion,
Deutsche Verlags-Anstalt, Stuttgart 1990: 81
Jan Vermeer, Arnhem (the big Aquarium): Inside cover
Hans Welreman/OMA, Rotterdam: 146 (photo)
Quist Wintermans Architecten, Rotterdam: 120 f.
(all drawings and coloured plan)
René de Wit: 91 (photo of model)
Zwarts & Jansma Architecten, Amsterdam: 127 f.

All not mentioned photos, drawings and sketches by ABT/Rob Nijsse.

The author would like to thank all photographers, architects and others
who supplied illustrations. Every effort was made to identify and quote
the copyright holders. Where this was not possible we ask the copyright
holders to contact ABT/Rob Nijsse.

Acknowledgements

The writing of a book is a rewarding but hideous task. What started as a good idea – to show the world the progress we have made regarding the structural use of glass – proved to be a three year labour comparable with the tasks set to the mythological hero Hercules such as cleaning the stalls of King Augias, finding the golden apples and fighting the lion and Amazon warriors. These are all metaphors for time consuming work, delay, unattainable information and lack of inspiration.

I spent long evenings and weekends at the table in the living room writing and sketching for this book. So I would like to thank my wife Ineke and my two sons Erik and Bart for putting up with a husband and a father who, sometimes, was there physically but not as a family member.

Special thanks are due to Bart for enduring the thankless task of being a test load on glass tables and glass panels.

Completing the text was one task, getting good pictures another, preparing the drawings yet a third. In this respect I would like to thank all the people who assisted me to assemble the required materials. The copyrights list contains their names.

Many of the drawings in this book were prepared at the ABT office. Special thanks go to the able draftsmen who worked out my sketches into technically correct drawings. Also I would like to thank my fellow directors, Jacques Hulsbergen, Ton Boerhof, Walter Spangenberg and Gerard Doos for giving me the space and the support not only to write this book but also to embark right from the start with the Sonsbeek pavilion in 1986 on the quest for the structural use of glass. This quest implies certain risks since we are exploring on the borders of technical knowledge and technical possibilities. The way we like to work at ABT, however, fits in this careful exploration of possibilities.

Last but not least I would like to thank Michael Wachholz for translating the text into German, my editors Andreas Müller and Sabine Bennecke at Birkhäuser Publishers for helping me to turn a collection of frivolous texts, nice pictures and pencil sketches into a professional book. They showed me the way to do things correctly and adjusted many details, improving the book in most cases. Accordingly I appreciate the work of Alexandra Zöller who is responsible for the graphic design. The result of the collaboration of a technically orientated person and an aesthetically orientated person proved to be more than the simple addition of the two aspects.

Arnhem, 17 june 2003

Rob Nijsse